Above Edinburgh

AND SOUTH-EAST SCOTLAND

Above Edinburgh

AND SOUTH-EAST SCOTLAND

ANGUS *and* PATRICIA MACDONALD

WITH ADDITIONAL RESEARCH BY DEBORAH MAWDSLEY

INTRODUCTION BY
Neal Ascherson

POEMS BY
Norman MacCaig

MAINSTREAM
PUBLISHING

ABOVE EDINBURGH AND SOUTH-EAST SCOTLAND ·

Copyright © Angus and Patricia Macdonald 1989

First published in Great Britain 1989 by
MAINSTREAM PUBLISHING COMPANY (EDINBURGH) LTD
7 Albany Street
Edinburgh EH1 3UG

ISBN 1 85158 236 3 (cloth)

British Library Cataloguing in Publication Data
Macdonald, Angus
Above Edinburgh and South-East Scotland.
1. South-east Scotland.   Description and travel
I. Title   II. Macdonald, Patricia
914.13'04858

Design and layout by James Hutcheson and Paul Keir
Typeset in 11/12 Garamond by Bookworm Typesetting Ltd, Edinburgh
Printed in Great Britain by Butler and Tanner Ltd, Frome, Somerset

For Donald A. Macdonald and Marjory J.H.S. Macdonald

ACKNOWLEDGEMENTS

We would like to thank warmly all those individuals and institutions who have helped us in the preparation of this book, particularly the following:

For involving us in the idea of the book, Tom Steel and Mike Scott of Radio Forth.

For generously given assistance with background information and/or checking of photographs and captions: Deborah Mays and Miles Oglethorpe of Historic Buildings and Monuments, Scotland; W.J. Baird, Ian Bunyan, David Caldwell, David Clarke, John Shaw and James Wood of the National Museums of Scotland; staff of the British Geological Survey (Edinburgh), particularly Nigel Fannin; Maria Chamberlain; David Chamberlain of the Royal Botanic Garden, Edinburgh.

We would like to express very special thanks to Deborah Mays for her tireless, constantly enthusiastic and highly expert help with background research. The book would have been very much the poorer without her extremely efficient and positive involvement.

Any errors which the book nevertheless contains are of course, despite the help of those mentioned above, entirely our own responsibility and any opinions expressed are solely our own.

For keeping us in the air, sometimes against great odds, the staff of Edinburgh Air Centre, especially George Lamb.

For help with photographic services, Norman Houston and Martin Baker of J. Lizars Ltd (Wholesale Department), the staff of Eastern Photocolour Ltd, especially Frank Cornfield and Alex Porteous, and the staff of Xpress Print Ltd.

For her efficiency in producing a beautiful clean typescript of the text in record time, and for her interest in its contents, Margaret Todd.

For all their involvement and hard work in initiating, editing and producing the book, the staff and associates of Mainstream Publishing, especially Bill Campbell, Anna Fenge, Peter MacKenzie, Dorothy Smith and Claire Watts.

For their excellent and imaginative work to an extremely tight schedule, the book's designers, James Hutcheson and Paul Keir.

For his understanding and enthusiastic encouragement of the project and for his deeply evocative and thought-provoking introduction (as well as for our enjoyment of many wise and interesting articles published elsewhere), Neal Ascherson of the *Observer*.

For his sympathetic interest and for kindly allowing us to use the wonderful poems which we have always seen as forming part of the book, Norman MacCaig, with his publishers, Chatto & Windus.

Acknowledgements are due to the following for permission to quote from material in their possession:

Penguin Books for extracts from *The Buildings of Scotland* (*Edinburgh* and *Lothian* volumes,by John Gifford, Colin McWilliam and David Walker and by Colin McWilliam respectively), Edinburgh University Press for extracts from *The Making of Classical Edinburgh* by Professor A.J. Youngson, Salamander Press for extracts from *Picturesque Notes* by Robert Louis Stevenson.

Angus and Patricia Macdonald, June 1989

SELECTED BIBLIOGRAPHY

Baird, W.J., *The Scenery of Scotland: The Structure Beneath*, National Museums of Scotland, Edinburgh, 1988.

Baldwin, J., *Exploring Scotland's Heritage, Lothians & Borders*, HMSO, Edinburgh, 1985.

Cant, M., *Villages of Edinburgh, Vol 1*, John Donald, Edinburgh, 1986.

Cameron, D.K., *The Ballad and the Plough*, Futura, London, 1979.

Catford, E.F., *Edinburgh, The Story of a City*, Hutchinson, London, 1975.

Cruden, S., *The Scottish Castle*, 3rd Edition, Spurbooks, Edinburgh, 1981.

Daiches, D., *Edinburgh*, Granada, London, 1978.

Daiches, D., *A Companion to Scottish Culture*, Edward Arnold, London, 1986.

Duckham, B.F., *A History of the Scottish Coal Industry, Vol. 1, 1700-1815*, David & Charles, Newton Abbot, 1970.

Drabble, M., & Lewinski, J., *A Writer's Britain: Landscape in Literature*, Thames & Hudson, London, 1979.

Dunbar, J.G., *The Architecture of Scotland*, 2nd Edition, Batsford, London, 1978.

Fenton, A., *Scottish Country Life*, John Donald, Edinburgh, 1976.

Fernie J., & Pitkethly, A.S., *Resources, Environment & Policy*, Harper & Row, London, 1986.

Gifford, J., *Buildings of Scotland, Fife*, Penguin Books, Harmondsworth, 1988.

Hendrie, W., *Discovering West Lothian*, John Donald, Edinburgh, 1986.

Kas, W., (Ed.), *Odyssey, Voices from Scotland's Past*, Polygon, Edinburgh, 1982.

Lamont-Brown, R., *Discovering Fife*, John Donald, Edinburgh, 1988.

Little, G.A., *Scotland's Gardens*, Spurbooks, Edinburgh, 1981.

MacCaig, Norman, *Collected Poems*, Chatto & Windus, London, 1985.

MacCaig Norman, *Voice-over*, Chatto & Windus, London, 1985.

Mackie, J.D., *A History of Scotland*, Penguin Books, Harmondsworth, 1969.

Maclean, C., *The Fringe of Gold*, Canongate, Edinburgh, 1985.

McWilliam, C., *Scottish Townscape*, Collins, London, 1975.

McWilliam, C., *Buildings of Scotland, Lothian*, Penguin Books, Harmondsworth, 1978.

McWilliam, C., Gifford, J., Walker, D., *Buildings of Scotland, Edinburgh*, Penguin Books, Harmondsworth, 1984.

Marshall, R.K., *Queen of Scots*, HMSO, Edinburgh, 1986.

Mitchison, R., *A History of Scotland*, 2nd Edition, Methuen, London, 1982.

Mair, C., *Mercat Cross & Tolbooth*, John Donald, Edinburgh, 1988.

New, A., *A Guide to the Abbeys of Scotland*, Constable, London, 1988.

Piggot, S., *Cairnpapple*, 2nd Edition, HMSO, Edinburgh, 1985.

Ritchie, G. & A., *Scotland: Archaeology and Early History*, Thames & Hudson, London, 1981.

Smout, T.C., *A History of the Scottish People, 1560-1830*, Collins, London, 1969.

Smout, T.C., *A Century of the Scottish People, 1830-1950*, Collins, London, 1986.

Steel, T., *Scotland's Story*, Fontana, London, 1984.

Tait, A.A., *The Landscape Garden in Scotland 1735-1835*, Edinburgh University Press, Edinburgh, 1980.

Walker, B. & Ritchie, G., *Exploring Scotland's Heritage, Fife & Tayside*, HMSO, Edinburgh, 1987.

Whittow, J.B., *Geology and Scenery in Scotland*, Penguin Books, Harmondsworth, 1979.

Whyte, Ian & Kathleen, *Discovering East Lothian*, John Donald, Edinburgh, 1988.

Youngson, A.J., *The Making of Classical Edinburgh*, Edinburgh University Press, Edinburgh, 1966.

CONTENTS

My Water of Leith runs through a double city;
My city is threaded by a complex stream.
A matter for regret. If these cold stones
Could be stones only, and this watery gleam
Within the chasms of tenements and the pretty
Boskage of Dean could echo the groans
Of cart-wheeled bridges with only water's voice,
October would be just October. The bones
Of rattling winter would still lie underground,
Summer be less than ghost, I be unbound
From all the choking folderols of choice.

from DOUBLE LIFE

INTRODUCTION
by Neal Ascherson

When I laid down the proofs, my first thought was: 'This is a Sacred Book'. Not in the sense that it expounds a doctrine or a cult, but in a wider way: this is like the book which in legends is dug up under some hill, containing pages in an unknown script and language. All recognise that here the secrets must lie; none can claim to be able to read them. As soon as you begin to turn through Patricia Macdonald's photographs, you will be aware of this combination of mystery and significance. All is here: the answer to how bracken, stones, man and sea are in spite of all appearances one. Sometimes, staring into these landscapes (which is already far too weak and partial a definition of these images), the secret seems about to open, or at least a light moves beyond the closed door. You are staring right at that answer, and it must be so simple. But nobody has deciphered it yet.

I kept returning to one illustration here. It shows Croy Hill near Kilsyth. It shows a bare moorland, on which can be seen a stretch of the Antonine Wall, a bing, a quarry, hundreds of fibre-fine human tracks and sheep tracks, a cold lochan or dub, a couple of withered trees. It is Scotland, but also a parable of the very special way in which the tribes which presently dwell there feel about their country. Most peoples, in their longing image of home, resort to 'nature': the Russians perhaps to birch trees, the Slovak to a mountain. Scotland, for most of its inhabitants, includes the mark of man in that 'nature'.

Would it be possible to imagine an empty Scotland, apart from that almost empty wilderness of the north and west? I mean: a land whose forests had not been felled, and where a few bands of men went warily to the river-crossing for fear of wolves and bears. There's an illusion which can be experienced, given the right weather, by looking across from St Monance or Pittenweem towards the southern shore of the Firth of Forth. Over there an almost uninhabited country is revealed. Arthur's Seat and the other basalt plug-hills can clearly be seen, but there is no city or town about them. The shore below North Berwick Law is empty. Far inland, the snowy sierras of this desolate place rise up. But usually there is one thread of smoke to be seen, ascending from some invisible hut. Over there is the land of the Votadini, who – when they get their act together – will raise some kind of citadel on the cliff above the Nor' Loch, and bury silver on Traprain Law, and endure the Romans, and learn from them how to make window-glass, and hang on long after the Romans have left, and become in the end – after defeat by the Anglians – refugees in another Celtic country which is now called Wales.

And all that they did and suffered has marked the place. In the end,

CROY HILL, CUMBERNAULD AND KILSYTH

The Antonine Wall traverses the photograph in the middle distance from right to left, a bing occupies the foreground and a quarry the background; the picture is an excellent example of the overlaying of human marks from different historical periods upon the landscape.

BORDER HILLS IN THE SNOW

after enjoying that view across the Firth, the most important thing in it turns out to be the thread of smoke. This cannot be Baffin Land or South Georgia. This is Scotland, where the human race and its work have become compounded with the land and the land's own blind changes. Look once more at these photographs, not only the rural but the urban ones. Is there a difference in quality between what a glacier did to a landscape half a million years ago and what a colliery did to it a hundred years ago? There is not, really, and in the same way the pattern of the Moray Estate on the ground of Edinburgh is related, not fancifully but directly, to that of sea-cliffs as the Bass Rock is related to the cathedral in Palmerston Place. As a child, I remember, I had difficulty understanding the distinction people made between a bridge like the Dean Bridge and a structure of living rock like that on which the Castle sits. I had apprehended them as in some sense the same, although knowing at some level that one was made of quarried blocks and the other was an obtrusion of the earth's bones. It was puzzling to think that bridge-builders were performing something antithetical to nature, 'subduing' or 'transcending' the natural creation. But that was the conventional, 'Faustian' view of the relationship of Man to World, accepted not only by Hegelians, Marxists and Fascists but by every adherent of the religion of progress, in the times when I was a child. We know better now.

As the Faustian world-view collapses, so the significance of Scotland's physical appearance grows. If there is one place in the world in which to understand the human place in creation, that secret of unity of the artificial and natural, planned and accidental, then it is here. And this book is a primer in that course of post-Faustian studies. If it is true, as this work demonstrates, that Scotland is supremely the place where the human race and the physical environment can be shown to belong together, to be part of one another . . . then why? Could it be connected, for instance, with this country's remarkable output of cosmologising geologists or geocosmologists, or whatever they could be called – Hugh Miller, Lyell, even Robert Chambers in his *Vestiges of Creation*? What's trying to express itself through a book-title like *Testimony of the Rocks*? Why should it be that the only great scoop in the enormous lifetime of *The Scotsman* should be to have scooped the Ice Age (the editor sent a reporter to follow Louis Agassiz round Scotland on his famous journey in 1840, when the great Swiss naturalist identified the scars of universal glaciation)?

Patricia and Angus Macdonald, with their art and learning, help us towards answering that 'why'. I can see two lines of explanation. One is geology: human settlement and activity take place as a sort of lichen in the less exposed crevices and surfaces of the land. The glaciers drive their U-shaped valleys down to the sea, and vanished rivers or flows of icewater deposit their fans or straths of sediment: sometimes boulders and gravel, sometimes fine stuff which will become fertile soil. The coal measures approach the surface, and there will be mines; the sea is shallow and in that place there may be salt-pans; the volcanoes explode, die and are worn away, leaving abrupt rocks for fortresses. There is not much room for unfettered planning in Scotland. Most communities are improvisations in strait circumstances, which is why the few examples of sovereign geometry in towns – the New Town, but some of the small Border places too – are so stirring.

A second line of explanation, closely related, is poverty. In many of these pictures the soil is shallow and acid, the rock pokes through the worn sleeve of the turf, erosion gullies run down from the hilltops, trees have short trunks and low canopies. This has been a hard country to live in, as it still is in many ways, and that is the fault of latitude, geology and geography. Scottish earth is in most places, even in the south, a skin over bone, and like any face it never loses a line once acquired. On these photographs every cut and dyke, every digging and rig, every hut-footing and posthole, fort-bank and cattle path, tractor-mark and lawn-mower swathe and chariot-rut, seems to have left its trace. By convention, air photography is said to reveal a 'palimpsest'. This is true, in the sense that on every page there is layer upon layer of time-writing. But palimpsests are supposed only to show the last surface and the latest message to the reader. In some of the Macdonalds' photographs in this book, the surface of Scotland shows every mark at once, from the first pencil-strokes of Bronze Age ploughland to the new bunker dug on the golf course last spring. Sometimes it is plain what these past events were. Often it is not. The photograph of Fettes school playing-fields, for example, shows the faintest shadows of some quite other use which is no longer identifiable.

But there is another way in which *Above Edinburgh* begins to open ultimate secrets. This is not just the effacing of the differences between animate and inanimate, the living and the unliving: a philosophical region which the poet Hugh MacDiarmid reached in some of the meditations of *On a Raised Beach*. These secrets are about the scale of things, about macro and micro. That astonishing photograph taken from directly above Moray Place was, when I first glanced at it, the view upwards into the cupola of a New Town stairwell. Then, in one moment of vertigo, I saw that the sky above was snow below, that the lights on the top-flat stairhead were the frontages of huge houses illuminated by sunset, that this object was a thousand times larger than I had appreciated. The Tay Bridge is a metal frill, the bay at Tantallon the face of a young man crying out in some violent passion. A fragment of worn-out crocodile leather is the summit of Arthur's Seat, and glittering droplets of water on it are climbers in white shirts. And these games with phenomenology, played so cunningly by Patricia Macdonald's camera in the sky, are more than games. They hint that being has either no scale, or an infinity of scales – the idea of infinitesimal universes within an atom, or of this earth as a particle revolving round some molecule in the backside of a monster made of trillions of such molecules.

Air photography, the book suggests, could justifiably make some big claims for itself. The little aircraft looks down as the Lord is implored to look down upon city, field, hill, sea-coast and ruin. It makes the work of farmers, soldiers and subterranean fires into abstract patterns; it dismisses a nuclear power station and raises up a tiny, derelict church instead; it bounces on thermals rising from factories, crematoria, the coal fires of the citizens or the funnels of locomotives.

And those images suggest a last discovery by the Macdonalds. Even modernity does not often defile: this is a country whose face is partly made of work and in which work can still turn into landscape. There are beauties in motorway embankments here, in new factories as well as in Victorian mills. Angus Macdonald's text doesn't always speak the same language as the pictures: he writes disapprovingly of the Savacentre at Cameron Toll as a 'shopping shed' belonging to the 'motor culture' but in the photograph the vast thing has all the mass of a mountainside. Even Patricia Macdonald's talent doesn't make New St Andrews House/the St James Centre any better than cultural murder – the sort of priggish, heartless, irreparable murder once inflicted by Covenanting extremists on their critics. But with that exception the Macdonalds have demonstrated that almost anything built on Scotland turns into Scotland.

This book means a lot, in every sense of the phrase. All that I have been trying to say about it is contained, one way or another, in the verses by Norman MacCaig which are printed here, and done better too. Any level of comment works with these photographs, from simple remembering to seeking history to political statements to philosophy. Perhaps the best way to praise the achievement of Patricia and Angus Macdonald is to say that they have seen the universality of Scotland, and made it possible for everyone else to perceive it too.

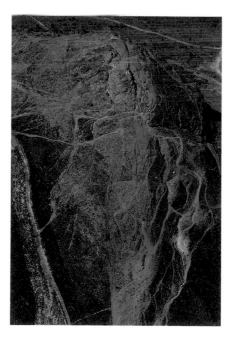

THE SUMMIT OF
ARTHUR'S SEAT,
EDINBURGH

When ever was there a beginning? –
Not of night and its furniture,
Its transcriptions, its cool décor;
Nor of thinking about it:
But when was there a beginning
Of this turbulent love
For a sea shaking with light
And a lullabying ditchwater
And a young twig being grave
Against constellations – these –
And people, invisibly webbing
Countries and continents,
Weeping, laughing, being idle
And always, always
Moving from light to darkness and
To light: a furniture
Of what? – a transcription, a décor
Of Being, that hard abstract
Curled in the jelly of an eye
And webbed through constellations
And cities and deserts, and frayed
In the wet feathers of treetops.

from NO END, NO BEGINNING

I

ANCIENT BEGINNINGS

MODERN SCOTLAND consists of that part of the British Isles which lies north of the Cheviot Hills and which came into being as a political entity in the medieval period. Of the people who occupied the land before this time little is known. The earliest inhabitants were hunter-gatherers who may have caused local damage to the environment by burning small areas of forest but who have left little trace of their existence. Around 3500 BC Neolithic people with a more settled form of life migrated north into the area. They were Scotland's first farmers and they are known to have used stone tools and to have made pottery. Their society appears to have been organised in such a way that people could be spared for large building projects and the main effort in this direction was put into sites which had ritual or burial functions rather than into domestic buildings. The earliest structures on Cairnpapple Hill, which date from approximately 3000 BC, were made by these people and the imposing circle of standing stones on this site, dating from around 2500 BC, shows evidence of a high degree of technical skill and knowledge; stone circles of this type appear to have had sophisticated functions not related only to the immediate vicinity of the site.

From around 1000 BC a change occurred in the nature of built forms which were large enough to have survived into the present day. The ramparts surrounding settlements, such as at 'The Chesters' fort near Drem in East Lothian, are the most substantial remains from this period, during which a need for displays of martial panoply seems to have become an important consideration in the deployment of building resources. By the time the Romans occupied southern Scotland in the first century AD, which they did for purely military reasons, native British tribes had evolved some very large settlements, such as those at the Eildon Hills and at Traprain Law, and these either remained occupied throughout the Roman period or were reoccupied following the Roman withdrawal. The fact that structures such as these are almost the only substantial ones to survive from this time does not, of course, mean that ritual and burial ceased to be important nor that settlements were not built during the earlier period, but rather that there had been a change in the ways in which these aspects of society were expressed. When looking at the traces remaining on the land of South-East Scotland from the periods before and after about 1000 BC, we should simply be aware that we are not comparing like with like.

CAIRNPAPPLE HILL, WEST LOTHIAN

Cairnpapple Hill north of Bathgate occupies a special place in southern Scotland because from here it is possible to see practically the whole of Fife and the Lothians, as well as northwards to Schiehallion and Ben Lomond and westwards to Goatfell on Arran. There is evidence that it was used for religious or funerary purposes from 3000 BC until the beginning of the Christian era and it is therefore one of the most important archaeological sites in Scotland. The pattern of usage was complicated. The first monument was an irregular arc of ritual holes visible here within the gravel circle. A second, outer, ring of holes is the remains of a henge or ring of stones which was apparently constructed around 500 years later when the rock-cut ditch and bank were also made. A third phase consisted of a large cairn (reconstructed) and a fourth of a substantial enlargement of this – the position of the base of the larger cairn is marked on the ground today by the gravel circle. The builders of the first cairn seem to have desecrated the henge and possibly even to have used the stones in building the cairn, which is just one of the remarkable features of the site and suggests a change of religious tradition. Throughout the whole of its period of use the hill seems to have been regarded as a sacred place, and was probably a focus of attention for prehistoric peoples for nearly 3000 years.

EILDON HILLS, ETTRICK AND LAUDERDALE

The group of three small hills known as the Eildons is one of the most prominent features of the eastern Border counties. It can be seen from most parts of the Lammermuir and Moorfoot Hills as well as from the Cheviots and the whole of the Merse. The three hills dominate the routes along the Tweed and Leader waters and important fords across the Tweed. Legend has it that they were cloven into three in a demonstration of the magical powers of the wizard Michael Scott.

Eildon Hill North was occupied in prehistoric times, possibly from the seventh century BC and has at one time evidently been the location of a considerable town. The slightly pock-marked appearance of the summit is caused by around 300 hut circles – level platforms on which timber-framed houses were built – which indicate a community of approximately 2,000 people. This could not have been self-sufficient which suggests that a complex society, involved with trade and industry as well as agriculture, existed here in prehistoric times.

In the first century AD the hill was used as a Roman signal station, part of the system of communications on the line of Dere Street which linked the northern Roman frontier with the south. The massive Roman fort of Newstead (Trimontium) lay half a mile to the north on the south bank of the Tweed.

'THE CHESTERS'
FORT, EAST
LOTHIAN

Hill-forts proliferated in South-East Scotland during the first millennium BC and some remained in use during and after the Roman occupation. In their final form they consisted of rings of ditches and ramparts surrounding a prominent location which could be easily defended. The absence of a water supply within most of them suggests that they were designed for protection against raiding parties rather than to withstand prolonged siege, but they do seem to have been permanently settled. Most underwent several stages of development, beginning as timber-palisaded enclosures and progressing to multiple-rampart systems of stone and earth. The switch from timber to stone may have resulted from a shortage of timber, and from single to multiple structures from changes in weapons technology.

Earlier settlements in this area were undefended and quite why these forts should have become necessary is still the subject of speculation. A likely explanation is, however, that an increasing population was exerting pressure on the available resources, such as easily-cultivated land, grazing and woodland, in a period when the climate was becoming colder and wetter. It has also been suggested that the complex multilple-rampart systems may have been intended for show rather than defence. The particular fort illustrated here lends credence to this theory because it is located in a vulnerable position, being overlooked by higher

ground nearby. If this theory is correct it would seem to indicate that pride and prestige were becoming increasingly important and that greater stratification of society was also occurring. As these are attributes which tend to develop when competition over territory exists, perhaps the pressure on resources was indeed responsible for this trend towards increasing militarism and pomp – a lesson which is surely relevant for us today.

EDINSHALL BROCH, BERWICKSHIRE

There are structures from several different periods on this site above the Whiteadder Water, but the most remarkable is Edinshall Broch, the circular-plan masonry dwelling which is clearly visible in the photograph, and which dates from the second century AD. This type of fortified building is associated with the cultures of northern Scotland and is very rare in the south. We can only speculate as to the circumstances which led to its construction here, but it may be that it was commissioned from professional broch builders by a leading Lowland family, to give them a measure of security against the Romans.

WODEN LAW, ROXBURGH

This view depicts the northern edge of the Cheviot Hills; the Cheviot itself is the snow-covered peak in the distance and in the foreground is Woden Law, whose top is protected by several lines of earthwork. Woden Law occupied a position of considerable strategic importance because a major highway linking northern and southern Britain, which was in use from pre-Roman times until the late medieval period and which was the Roman Dere Street, passes close by. Native British settlements occupied this hill before and after the Romans, but seem to have been cleared from it during the Roman period, no doubt for reasons of security. It is believed that the Romans used the hill for army training. They appear to have built several of the earthworks and to have made platforms for siege engines.

TRAPRAIN LAW, EAST LOTHIAN

When the Romans arrived in South-East Scotland they found it occupied by a tribe which they called the Votadini, whose territory included what are now the Lothians and the Berwickshire Merse, and whose capital seems to have been a settlement of considerable size – equivalent to that on the Eildon Hills – at Traprain. It is an ideal site, being visible as a symbol of power from most of East Lothian and also from the numerous hill-forts on the northern edge of the Lammermuirs. Occupation seems to have been continuous from around 700 BC until the fifth century AD and was at its height around 300 AD. The fact that this site remained occupied throughout the Roman period suggests that the Votadini enjoyed good relations with the foreign power and in fact the complete absence of Roman remains east of Dere Street, indicates that the Votadini lands were not policed by the Romans.

Excavations on the site have shown that, at its peak, Traprain must have been a substantial settlement; perhaps the most intriguing find there was a hoard of silver, which was probably buried in the fifth century AD, now in the collections of the National Museums of Scotland. This was Roman in origin but was clearly some form of booty as many of the items (cups, plates and bowls) had been flattened or cut up ready for the melting pot. We can only speculate as to the circumstances surrounding its burial. It may have been plundered from a wealthy Roman settlement further south, but the explanation currently favoured by archaeologists is that the loot was acquired legitimately from the Romans, by a chief, for political or military services rendered by the tribe.

HIGH STREET, EDINBURGH

Here's where to make a winter fire of stories
And burn dead heroes to keep your shinbones warm,
Bracing the door against the jackboot storm
With an old king or two, stuffing the glories
Of rancid martyrs with their flesh on fire
Into the broken pane that looks beyond Fife
Where Alexander died and a vain desire,
Hatched in Macbeth, sat whittling at his life.

Across this gulf where skeins of duck once clattered
Round the black Rock and now a tall ghost wails
Over a shuddering train, how many tales
Have come from the hungry North of armies shattered,
An ill cause won, a useless battle lost,
A head rolled like an apple on the ground;
And Spanish warships staggering west and tossed
On frothing skerries; and a king come to be crowned.

Look out into this brown November night
That smells of herrings from the Forth and frost;
The voices humming in the air have crossed
More than the Grampians; East and West unite,
In dragonish swirlings over the city park,
Their tales of deaths and treacheries, and where
A tall dissolving ghost shrieks in the dark
Old history greets you with a Bedlam stare.

He talks more tongues than English now. He fetches
The unimagined corners of the world
To ride this smoky sky, and in the curled
Autumnal fog his phantoms move. He stretches
His frozen arm across three continents
To blur this window. Look out from it. Look out
From your November. Tombs and monuments
Pile in the air and invisible armies shout.

II

MEDIEVAL AND
RENAISSANCE

THE PICTURE which we can piece together of the life and culture of any past age from the buildings and other structures which it created, will always be a distorted one because only the most substantial and durable of these remain. In dealing with the medieval period in Scotland, we must therefore compose our view from castles, from ecclesiastical buildings (cathedrals and monasteries), of which substantial fragments remain to us, and from the buildings which formed parts of the old burghs. In fact, very little of what is seen today in a Scottish burgh is a true survival from the medieval period, but because much of the subsequent rebuilding preserved the older patterns of streets and wynds the structure at least of the original can still be discerned. Of the insubstantial buildings in which most people lived, nothing now remains above ground.

King David I (1124-53), who was perhaps the most energetic of the Canmore kings, introduced feudalism into southern Scotland and with this came a system of government which was quite different from what had existed before. Previously, the social and political structure had been tribal; the bond which held together the societies which had built the hillforts and other settlements, seen in the previous chapter, was one of kinship. David established the ideas of military feudalism and a central royal government. The implications were that all land was considered to be royal land and that all authority resided in the king. The king made grants of land to his nobles and with this went certain responsibilities: the noble was required to maintain a castle to help the king to keep civil order and was expected to present himself with his followers, suitably armed, in time of war. The 'ordinary' people were granted permission from the noble to cultivate land and in return owed him a duty of service, and were obliged to make payments to him in the form of agricultural produce. They expected also to receive the lord's protection; the proper role of the feudal lord's establishment was to keep the peace, administer justice, and, in an age before insurance companies or a welfare state, to offer material assistance to any individual who might be overcome by personal or domestic disaster. The extent to which any of this actually operated in practice is, of course, open to question. The essential change which occurred under David by the introduction of feudalism was, however, that social and political allegiances were now related to homage for land occupied rather than to respect for blood ties. This had the effect of bringing practically the whole of what is present-day Scotland under a single royal jurisdiction and therefore resulted in a new form of political stability for the emerging nation.

The feudal system was established first in South-East Scotland principally by the granting of land by the king to immigrants from

England and French Flanders (a process which is sometimes referred to as the 'Normanisation' of Scotland) and it resulted in the creation of social and political structures which were similar to those of the rest of Europe. The massive castles of the medieval period are the principal physical remnants of this system. A further force for stability and coherence was the reorganisation of the church on a diocesan system with parishes, which produced a uniform style of worship. Encouragement of the monastic orders, particularly by David I, was also important; the monks introduced new ideas in agriculture, and in mineral extraction – principally coal – and in embryo industries such as salt-making. The cathedrals and monasteries which survive in the landscape remind us of their contribution to these changes.

The medieval period was also the time in which the earliest Scottish Royal Burghs were founded. These were towns whose inhabitants were granted by royal charter the right to trade abroad and to hold fairs and markets. Each burgh had an exclusive right to trade, a monopoly in other words, within a defined surrounding area called the burgh's 'liberty'. Anything sold within the 'liberty' had either to have been made by the burgh's craftsmen or to have had a duty tax paid at the burgh, if it came from elsewhere. On the East Coast especially, burghs became centres of international trade, the gateways through which luxury goods such as wine, spices and fine cloth entered the country. These were paid for by exporting surpluses of agricultural produce (wool, occasionally grain), industrial products (coal, salt, hides) and other commodities such as salted fish.

The burghs were established by, and important to, the Crown both as sources of revenue – approximately one-sixth of the royal income came from taxes on burghs – and also as groupings of loyal subjects. It was in the interests of a burgh to support the king, otherwise he might revoke its charter and with that its right to trade. The burghs also had a vested interest in maintaining order because this was good for business.

The end of the Canmore dynasty in 1286, caused by the double family misfortune of the accidental death of Alexander III and the subsequent death of the infant Maid of Norway, who was by that time his sole heir, brought about a period of instability. There were the Wars of Independence from England (1286-1371), which were fought initially against Edward I, who claimed sovereignty over Scotland. Edward proved to be a brutal enemy whose armies wreaked havoc in the newly created burghs and monasteries, some of which never recovered their former prosperity. These wars should have been brought to an end by the Scottish victory at the Battle of Bannockburn (1314) but they were prolonged by ineffectual government. Their principal effect was that they united the young Scottish nation, particularly against the English.

The threat from England finally waned around the end of the fourteenth century, but nevertheless, through the fifteenth century, the times remained very unsettled, with much feuding and lawlessness, involving both the Crown and the Baronage. This resulted in a further spate of castle-building which has left us with these monuments to this particular period of folly. The power of the barons was finally controlled by the Crown, and the burghs played a role in this because they could normally be relied upon to side with the king against the baronage for the reasons already stated. Many burghs were created by various monarchs in the fifteenth and sixteenth centuries, largely for political reasons, and they are therefore physical indicators of the conditions of this period.

The sixteenth and seventeenth centuries, though bloody – a time of upheaval caused by such events as the Reformation and the Civil War – nevertheless saw a gradual increase in stability and in prosperity in Scotland with a consequent increase in the quality of civilised living for the ruling class. The Reformation, though it caused much strife and suffering as it progressed to what was finally to become an independent and highly democratically organised form of religion which was relatively immune from direct abuse by the rich and powerful, did not actually affect the look of the landscape significantly. It was a factor in the destruction of some fine buildings, such as the Border abbeys and the Cathedral of St Andrews, and caused the erection of some churches which were not without architectural merit, but, considering its influence on the life of the nation, its effect on the appearance of the land was slight.

The sixteenth and seventeenth centuries saw a gradual strengthening of ties with England; England's role as a Protestant political ally, if not 'soul mate', was a factor in this, and the political merging process of the two nations was brought about first by the Union of the Crowns in 1603 and finally by the Union of Parliaments in 1707. The second half of the seventeenth century was in many ways an era of important cultural advance for Scotland; it was a time when the influence of the Renaissance was felt strongly, the new ideas coming particularly through France and the Low Countries, and marks on the landscape in the shape of many fine buildings bear witness to this.

DIRLETON CASTLE, EAST LOTHIAN

Dirleton Castle is an example of a feudal power centre. The original stronghold was built by the wealthy Anglo-Norman de Vaux family which came to Scotland in the twelfth century under the patronage of David I as part of the process of feudalisation. The existing castle dates from the thirteenth century when the donjon was linked by a curtain wall to four other towers to make a castle of enclosure, in which form it became a complete baronial residence, capable of independent defence.

HAILES CASTLE, EAST LOTHIAN

Hailes Castle sits on a steep rocky outcrop above the river Tyne south-east of East Linton. The structure visible today was built as a castle of enclosure in the fourteenth century during the castle-building boom precipitated by the Wars of Independence, and, due to its location on the overland route between Edinburgh and the South, became involved in most of the lawlessness of the succeeding three centuries.

During the 'Rough Wooing' of 1544-49, when an attempt was made to confirm the betrothal of the infant Mary, Queen of Scots to the boy prince Edward VI, it was garrisoned by the English and probably for this reason escaped destruction. Other places were not so fortunate, however, and during this campaign the English laid waste five Scottish burghs, including Edinburgh, seven monasteries and 243 villages as well as crops, barns and windmills. The operation was unsuccessful however: in 1548 Mary was sent to France where she was subsequently married to the Dauphin, which was part of the price exacted by the French for helping to expel the English.

Hailes Castle was finally devastated by Cromwell's army in 1650.

TANTALLON CASTLE, EAST LOTHIAN

Tantallon was one of the last great tower and curtain-wall castles of South-East Scotland. Built in the fourteenth century it had a justifiable reputation for impregnability and more than once allowed its occupiers to defy the Crown in that troubled period of Scottish history, in the early sixteenth century, when the Baronage was uncontrollably powerful. Both James IV and James V laid siege to the castle, but neither was able to capture it by force. Towards the end of its occupied life in 1651, it was overcome only with great difficulty by Cromwell's forces in an age when this type of military architecture had long been rendered obsolete by the development of artillery.

NEIDPATH CASTLE, TWEEDDALE
Above right
BORTHWICK CASTLE, MIDLOTHIAN

Neidpath and Borthwick Castles are examples of that most Scottish of fortified residences, the tower-house. Curtain-wall castles such as Dirleton or Tantallon were lived in by the wealthiest, most powerful subjects of the Crown and were expensive both to build and maintain. Lesser gentry – ordinary lairds who possessed only modest means – developed the tower-house to provide a secure residence which allowed them nevertheless to live in a style which they considered appropriate to their position.

In the tower-house the essential accommodation of a baronial establishment

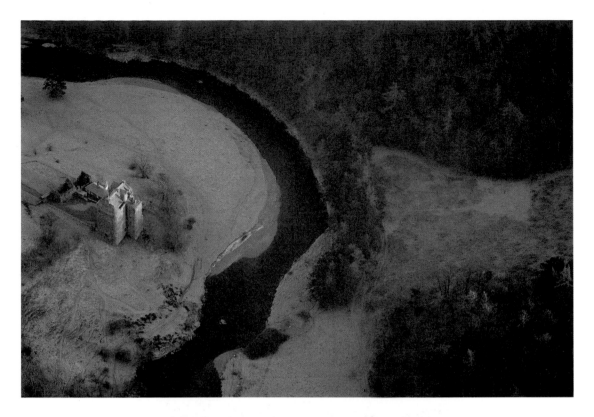

was reduced in scale and stacked vertically so that it could be packed into a single building with a small ground plan. All the features of the feudal castle were present but in miniature: the largest space would be the great hall, complete with kitchen and pantry at the 'low' end and lord's chamber, accessible from the 'high' end, usually on the floor above and connected by means of a turnpike stair. Storage space was placed on the lowest floors and sleeping accommodation for important members of the household in the highest. Lesser rooms were frequently located within the very thick walls.

The internal planning of these buildings was often carried out with great ingenuity and they provided the lairds of Scotland with residences which were secure, economical and not without pretension. The building type lasted well into the seventeenth century as the most popular form of house for country gentry in Scotland, long after fortified residences had been abandoned in favour of classical houses elsewhere in Europe.

EDINBURGH CASTLE – ST MARGARET'S CHAPEL

The oldest building in Edinburgh is the tiny St Margaret's Chapel, situated on the topmost point of the Castle Rock and visible here in the centre of the picture above the circular roof. Probably founded by David I, son of Margaret I and Malcolm III (Canmore), in the twelfth century, this is one of the earliest surviving examples of Norman architecture in Scotland.

It was Malcolm and Margaret Canmore who founded the dynasty under which Scotland was united politically and David I played a part in this by introducing feudalism to the country – the so-called 'Normanisation' of Scotland. The reform of the church, which Margaret began by convening councils of native clergy and establishing a coherent unity of practice, was second only to feudalism in the depth of its social impact.

DUNFERMLINE ABBEY, FIFE

Malcolm III (Canmore) built a fortress in Dunfermline in 1065 and made the town his place of residence. In 1069 the Saxon princess Margaret came here to be married to Malcolm and thus the Canmore dynasty, under which the old Celtic and Pictish group of kingdoms became transformed into a new Anglo-Norman realm, was founded. At Margaret's behest a Benedictine Priory was established in 1072 and this was subsequently elevated to an abbey in 1128 under David I. Margaret was buried here and the place became famous throughout the Christian world following her canonisation in 1250.

ST ANDREWS, FIFE

St Andrews was the ecclesiastical capital of Scotland during the medieval period. According to legend, the bones of the Apostle Andrew were brought here in the ninth century, after which it became a place of pilgrimage. A burgh was created some time between 1140 and 1155 to provide an income for the religious foundation and the cathedral itself was begun in 1160; the church was one of the largest in Britain, being second only to Norwich in length. For added security a castle, called the Bishop's Palace, was founded in 1200. It was a courtyard castle but the sixteenth century remains visible today have a Renaissance character more in keeping with a palace than a fortress. The bishops made St Andrews a centre of learning and the University was founded in 1413.

St Andrews was a focus of great activity in medieval times; the town and university remain today, but the great ecclesiastical see has gone; the cathedral was vandalised and stripped of its treasures in 1559 by a mob inflamed by a sermon of John Knox, and then it was allowed simply to crumble away.

MELROSE ABBEY, ETTRICK AND LAUDERDALE

Melrose Abbey was founded in 1136 by David I who granted it large areas of land and forest in the surrounding areas. Subsequent royal patronage in the twelfth and thirteenth centuries made it one of the richest monastic houses in Scotland.

The twelfth-century abbey was small and plain as befits the austerity of the Cistercian Order but it was sacked and destroyed by the English armies during the Wars of Independence. The monastery was rebuilt from the late fourteenth century on a grand scale and now represents the climax of Scottish Gothic architecture. Both French and English influences can be seen in the treatment of the ornamentation which contains versions of both the Decorated and Perpendicular styles.

DRYBURGH ABBEY, ETTRICK AND LAUDERDALE

Often considered the most romantic of the Border abbeys, Dryburgh is certainly the most picturesque. It was founded in 1150 and its early history was similar to that of Melrose; it received many grants of land together with churches during the first century of its existence and the need to administer these tended to destroy the primitive simplicity of the foundation. It suffered much during the Wars of Independence and in the later Border troubles associated with the 'Rough Wooing' of 1544 and with the Reformation. It then became the hereditary property of various landed proprietors and ceased to have any religious function from the end of the sixteenth century, after which its lands formed a source of wealth for entirely secular purposes.

The Abbey is the burial place of Sir Walter Scott.

INCHCOLM, FIFE

Inchcolm is an island in the Firth of Forth off Aberdour. An Augustinian Priory was founded here in 1123 and became an Abbey in 1235. It is the best preserved of Scotland's medieval monasteries despite having received the attentions of pirates and enemy warships at various times. Mass was last said here in 1560, the date which is usually taken as that of the Scottish Reformation.

The industrial installation in the background of this photograph is the Braefoot Bay Marine Terminal from which liquefied natural gas from the North Sea oilfield is shipped world-wide following processing at the plant at Mossmoran, four miles inland.

ST MARY'S CHURCH, HADDINGTON, EAST LOTHIAN

The original church on this site was granted as an appendage to the Priory of St Andrews by David I in 1134 along with lands, chapels and tithe. The present building was built in the late fourteenth and early fifteenth centuries during a period of stability and prosperity which produced many fine buildings in Scotland, and is perhaps the most impressive of the late medieval burgh kirks. It was completed over a fairly short period and has not been altered substantially since, so it has a rare consistency of style. It was badly damaged in the siege of Haddington of 1548-49 when the English garrisoned the town and held it against the Franco-Scottish army during the 'Rough Wooing' campaign. The

church, being outside the ramparts, was used by French and Scottish sharpshooters and this caused it to be wrecked by cannonfire from within the town. The nave was rebuilt in the sixteenth century and the choir restored in the 1970s.

ROSSLYN, MIDLOTHIAN

Rosslyn, which means the 'rock on the falls', is a magical place, thought by some to be similar in its associations to Glastonbury in England. It has a fifteenth-century castle, part of which is still inhabited, and, visible at the top of the picture, the most remarkable church in the country. Rosslyn Chapel, a collegiate church (i.e. a church with its own college of secular clergy) dating from the mid-fifteenth century, is unusual for the extraordinary richness of its ornamentation; every part of the interior is encrusted with deep carving which is in complete contrast to the plain severity normally found in Scottish buildings of the period. The most remarkable feature is the 'Prentice Pillar' which incorporates four strands of 'foliage' each starting from one of the base corners and spiralling through 180 degrees to the top.

All the great literary romantics of Scotland, including Byron and Scott, have found a place in their writings for Rosslyn.

GREYFRIARS CHURCH, EDINBURGH

Greyfriars Church is so called because a Franciscan Friary, founded in 1230, once occupied a site nearby. This was dissolved in 1490 and the lands were granted to the magistrates and town council of Edinburgh in 1562. A new parish church was built in 1602-20. This was a simple Protestant 'preaching box' and constitutes the eastern half of the present building. It quickly became a place in which history was made; the National Covenant – Scotland's declaration that it wished to remain Protestant – was signed here in 1638.

A completely new church with a separate congregation was built against the west wall at the beginning of the eighteenth century and the two churches existed together for many years. They were not finally united until the 1930s when the whole building was reconstructed.

GIFFORD CHURCH,
EAST LOTHIAN
*The present village of
Gifford dates from the
late seventeenth century.
Its main street is
dominated by a fine
example of a post-
Reformation T-plan kirk.
Possibly by James Smith,
an architect who is less
well remembered than he
deserves to be and who
built the Canongate
Church in Edinburgh, it
was constructed in 1710
shortly after the village
was moved to its present
site to allow the policies of
nearby Yester House to
be extended.*

41

DIRLETON VILLAGE, EAST LOTHIAN

Villages were a rarity in medieval Scotland where rural settlements usually took the form of scattered cottages or small hamlets. This may have been due to the emphasis on pastoral farming which did not require such extensive co-operation between neighbours as arable farming, or it may simply have been the result of the land not being particularly fertile and therefore unable to support large concentrated communities. East Lothian is one of the few parts of Scotland in which villages of ancient origin are found and Dirleton is thought to be one of them.

HADDINGTON, EAST LOTHIAN

Haddington was founded as a Royal Burgh by David I some time between 1124 and 1153. For a time it was a royal residence – Alexander II was born there in 1158 – but for most of its life it has been simply the principal market town and administrative centre of East Lothian.

The layout of Haddington is typical of a medieval Scottish burgh. At the centre was a large market place, the plan of which was an elongated triangle whose apex pointed westwards towards the burgh's common grazing at Gladsmuir. The market place was completely open *originally but was subsequently built up, first with temporary market stalls and finally with permanent buildings to form the triangular arrangement of streets which is seen today. Against the long sides of the triangle long narrow building plots – called 'burgages' – ran back to the burgh boundary. Each was possessed by one of the burghers who built a house at the end next to the market place and used the remainder as a garden or smallholding. Although these plots have subsequently been built upon, this original arrangement is clearly discernible in the view shown.*

CRAIL, FIFE

Crail received its Royal Charter from Robert I (Robert the Bruce) in 1310 and like Haddington is an example of a typical Scottish townscape. Most of the buildings have harled masonry walls and pantiled or slated roofs, and they occupy narrow plots of land which stretch back to form long gardens. During the sixteenth century Crail was one of Scotland's gateways to the continent of Europe and maintained a flourishing trade with the delta of Scheldt, the Norwegian fjords, the Danish Sound and the Low Countries. It therefore fulfilled the principal intended role of a Royal Burgh which was to generate revenue for the Crown from peaceable pursuits.

PITTENWEEM, FIFE
*Now the centre of Fife's
fishing industry,
Pittenweem originated as
a trading seaport. It
received its Royal
Charter in 1541 and like
Crail carried on a
flourishing trade with the
Baltic and the Low
Countries. The picture
shows many examples of
vernacular town
architecture with harled
walls, steeply pitched*

*pantiled or slated roofs
and wall-head gables
facing the street. Pantiles
were imported initially
but from the eighteenth
century were made
locally. They were
considered inferior to
slate and were not used
for the roofs of dwelling
houses until the
nineteenth century when
they replaced turf and
thatch on poorer
properties.*

THE ROYAL MILE, EDINBURGH

The Royal Mile of Edinburgh, stretching from the Castle to Holyrood, is the backbone of the Old Town. In fact there were two 'old towns' because the burgh of Edinburgh, which received its Royal Charter in 1124, extends only halfway from the Castle to Holyrood, the lower half of the street being in the separate burgh of Canongate, which was founded in 1143 and was only united with Edinburgh as recently as 1856. This famous street has formed a background against which most of the prominent figures of Scotland's past have enacted some part of their destiny.

Most of what is seen today in the Royal Mile, which comprises Castlehill, the Lawnmarket, the High Street and the Canongate, dates from the nineteenth century, but the underlying pattern of the street and its adjoining closes and wynds, as well as the forms of the buildings, are mainly medieval in origin, and this gives the place a slightly 'misplaced-in-time' quality. It accounts, for example, for the rather 'cardboard' appearance of St Giles Cathedral, which was heavily 'restored' in 1829-33.

OLD EDINBURGH

Down the Canongate
down the Cowgate
go vermilion dreams
snakes' tongues of bannerets
trumpets with words from their mouths
saying *Praise me, praise me.*

Up the Cowgate
up the Canongate
lice on the march
tar on the amputated stump
Hell speaking with the tongue of Heaven
a woman tied to the tail of a cart.

And history leans by a dark entry
with words from his mouth
that say *Pity me, pity me*
but never forgive.

CULROSS, FIFE

Culross became a Royal Burgh in 1592 and although its street pattern has been much altered it has a layout similar to Haddington and Crail. One of its most prominent buildings is the rather pretentiously named 'Culross Palace' which was the mansion of Sir George Bruce, one of the town's wealthiest proprietors, and which can be seen in the bottom left of the picture. Between 1590 and 1625 Bruce established a coal-mining and salt-making industry at Culross from which he made a personal fortune. This was part of the revolutionary expansion of Scottish coal production which occurred between 1550 and 1700 during which many small collieries were created in West Fife and the Lothians, with salt-works normally attached to those on the coast. It was an important development for the Scottish economy because an export trade developed to both England and the continent of Europe which improved Scotland's ability to import luxury goods from France and the Low Countries. It is an example of the type of innovation which would ultimately alter once again the balance of political power in Scotland, because once landowners began to exploit the mineral resources on their estates they became richer and more powerful with respect to the Crown and the burghs than they had been in the early medieval period. The era in which the landowners would become a very wealthy class, build for themselves large country houses and wield considerable political power was about to begin.

At the other end of the social scale the plight of the coal- and salt-workers was desperate. The work was so unpleasant that it became difficult to recruit labour and in 1608 the Scottish Parliament sanctioned the virtual enslavement of coal and salt-workers and their families. From that time colliers could be bought and sold with their pits and moved from pit to pit at the owners' whim. They were advertised for sale regularly in the Edinburgh newspapers.

As might be expected conditions did not improve under serfdom. The work was hard, dangerous and degrading and was carried out by men, women and children alike. Miscarriages were frequent and it was not unknown for women to give birth in a field next to the pit head.

Serfdom was not abolished in the Scottish coal industry until 1799. It therefore continued well into the period which is known as the 'Scottish Enlightenment'.

WINTON HOUSE, EAST LOTHIAN
Below left
Winton House was the mansion of the Earls of Winton, whose prosperity was based largely on the profits from their mines and salt-pans, clustered on the coast of East Lothian in the vicinity of Cockenzie and Prestonpans. Originally a tower-house, the building was enlarged and embellished in 1620-27 under William Wallace, who also worked on Heriot's Hospital and Holyrood Palace in Edinburgh. The design was an innovative one because Winton was one of the earliest large houses in Scotland in which an attempt was made to create an architectural effect as well as a functional building. Indigenous elements such as crowsteps and steeply pitched roofs were combined here with Anglo-Dutch features such as strapwork pediments, ogival turrets and barley-sugar chimney stacks, which shows that the influence of the Renaissance had finally percolated to northern Britain. If one had to put a name to this style it might be 'Anglo-Scots Renaissance'. Much of the seventeenth-century work on the exterior of Winton was obscured by later additions of around 1805 under John Paterson, which accounts for the rather plain look of the facade illustrated.

LINLITHGOW PALACE, WEST LOTHIAN
Above left
Linlithgow Palace, built in four stages between 1425 and 1620, is also a revolutionary design. It consists of four high ranges which form a square courtyard – a simple, symmetrical plan which was unique in medieval Scotland. The architecture is said to be of the 'Court School': it is transitional between military and domestic and marks the beginning of a new age. Although some defensive features were retained, the building is definitely a palace rather than a castle; it has large, regularly placed windows, spacious state apartments and a sophisticated and well organised system of communications consisting of stairs, corridors and lobbies. The planning shows Renaissance influence and the proto-classical ornamentation is Anglo-French in character.

Linlithgow Palace was the birthplace of Mary, Queen of Scots.

GEORGE HERIOT'S HOSPITAL, EDINBURGH

George Heriot's Hospital, which is in the foreground of this picture, was built between 1628 and 1700. It was the first of Edinburgh's several merchant schools; these were originally charity schools endowed by city merchants for the education of disadvantaged children such as orphans. They are now mostly independent fee-paying day schools.

George Heriot's is the prime example of the transition from the pure Scottish vernacular of the tower-house to Scottish Renaissance architecture and many foreign influences can be detected in the planning, which suggests that trade between Scotland and the continent of Europe was flourishing in this period. The plan is thought to have come from Serlio's Seventh Book of Architecture, *published in Italy around 1550, but the corner-tower arrangement is reminiscent of the large country houses of the English Renaissance. Much of the detailing, such as the strapwork ornamentation and the 'ogee' roofs, is Netherlandish, but the building nevertheless retains a Scottish flavour. The steeply pitched roofs, the verticality of the elevations, the crowsteps, the turreted towers and the turnpike stairs in the corners of the quadrangle are definitely Scottish elements.*

KINROSS HOUSE, KINROSSHIRE

Kinross House was built between 1679 and 1693 by the architect Sir William Bruce, for his own use. It is a truly classical building, being symmetrically arranged in both plan and elevation and having an hierarchical layout of rooms. The garden is formalised in response to the architecture so that building and landscape share a common axis aligned on a prominent distant feature – Loch Leven Castle – which is an unmistakeable hallmark of Bruce. Bruce was Scotland's first truly classical architect. His buildings had compact symmetrical plans, matching elevations ornamented with the classical Orders, and an austere quality, devoid of affectation, which was peculiarly Scottish.

THE PALACE OF HOLYROODHOUSE, EDINBURGH

Holyrood Palace is possibly remembered more for the dark deeds with which it was associated than for the pageantry which occurred and still does occur there, as the disappearing roll of red carpet shows. An abbey was founded here in 1128 by David I and the remains of this are seen in the top left of the picture above the single tower of the old Scots-Renaissance palace, built in 1528-32. A matching tower was added in 1671-76 and the two linked by a screen containing the main entrance to form a symmetrical composition, when the palace was extended under the direction of the architect Sir William Bruce. As with all Bruce's buildings, classicism is supreme here but the courtyard arrangement with entrance screen and the roofscape with dormer windows and prominent chimney stacks are French in origin.

'Great people of yore, kings and queens, buffoons and grave ambassadors, played their stately farce for centuries in Holyrood. Now all these things of clay are mingled with dust, the king's crown itself is shown for sixpence to the vulgar; but the stone palace has outlived these changes.'

— Robert Louis Stevenson

EARLY SUNDAY MORNING, EDINBURGH

Crosshatch of streets: some waterfall
Down pits, some rear to lay their forepaws
On hilly ledges; others bore
Tunnels through lilac, gean and holly.

A stretch of sky makes what it can
Of ships sailing and sailing islands.
Trees open their rustling hands
And toss birds up, a fountain, a fanfare.

A yellow milkcart clipclops by
Like money shaken in a box,
Less yellow than the golden coxcomb
Gallanting on St Giles's spire.

And people idle into space
And disappear again in it –
Apparitions from nowhere: unseen
Distances shine from their faces.

And, fore and hindpaws out of line,
An old dog mooches by, his gold
Eyes hung down below hunched shoulders,
His tail switching, feathery, finely.

III

EDINBURGH IN THE EIGHTEENTH CENTURY

IT IS REMARKABLE that Edinburgh, which at the beginning of the eighteenth century was something of a cultural backwater in European terms, should by its end have been able to boast that it was one of the intellectual capitals of the western world, a claim which people outside Scotland were prepared to accept as being not entirely fanciful. It is certainly true that a small number of native-born Scots based in Edinburgh in the eighteenth century made significant contributions to the development of the western intellectual tradition; David Hume's *Treatise of Human Nature* and Adam Smith's *Wealth of Nations* were two books which were enormously influential and which played crucial roles in the creation of twentieth-century materialism. Other thinkers, such as Adam Fergusson, a founder of modern sociology, and William Robertson, one of the first historians to work from original sources, made Edinburgh famous in the eighteenth century as a centre of scholarship, learning and literary prowess.

It has been suggested, somewhat mischievously, that the improvement in the quality of thinking which occurred in Edinburgh in the eighteenth century was caused by the departure of a large proportion of the aristocracy, who migrated south to London when it became the centre of Scottish as well as English political life after the Union of Parliaments in 1707. Perhaps a more likely explanation was the fact that by this time the educational objective of the otherwise in many ways infamous John Knox, which was that every parish in Scotland should have a school, was at last being realised. An Act of Parliament had been passed in 1696 requiring that every parish establish a school and pay for a schoolmaster and a significant proportion of Scottish children were receiving some kind of elementary education by the early eighteenth century. The most gifted of them were going on to study at the Scottish universities, which, unlike those in most other countries at this period, were willing to accept students from any background provided they were sufficiently able. It is a fact, however, that the well-known figures of the Scottish Enlightenment were drawn mainly from the moneyed classes. Presumably they had the time and leisure to devote to a financially unrewarding life of learning.

The principal architectural legacy of the period in South-East Scotland was the first New Town of Edinburgh. With its two great squares dedicated to St Andrew and Queen Charlotte and its wide streets, this was neo-classical in concept, the straight lines and symmetrical, rectilinear planning symbolising and testifying to a belief in the power of rational thinking and producing a townscape which was a fitting monument to the Age of Reason.

To begin with, the New Town was entirely residential, an 'ideal' city of grand houses in squares and principal streets, and more humble abodes in lesser streets. It was a speculative development initiated by an enlightened town council which recognised the need for the burgh to expand, purchased the necessary land and set up the administrative framework required to stimulate and then control the building process. The layout was designed by James Craig, a little-known architect for whom it is the only claim to fame, and the houses themselves were built out of private capital on separately feued (leased) building plots. They have a certain uniformity, due to the stipulations of the plan, which required that all houses conform to the same street line and roof height and possess certain other characteristics. Many features were left to the discretion of the individual builders, however, and this combination of conditions produced the variety within regularity which is one of the most endearing qualities of this part of the city.

The spacious layout of the New Town, which afforded such an abundance of fresh air, was no doubt enjoyed by the well-to-do Edinburgh residents who moved into it away from the relative squalor of the Old Town. It had, of course, been the overcrowding and unhealthy conditions of the Old Town which had provided the impetus for the building of the New Town, but the departure of the better-off did not significantly ease the problem of overcrowding, because the continuing migration of people from country to town, which was happening all over Europe at this time and which had been accelerated in Scotland due to the added momentum which the union with England in 1707 gave to the Scottish economy, caused the population of the Old Town to increase steadily. Conditions eventually became so bad that the health of the whole city was threatened and this provided the stimulus for the various public health and housing measures which were to be a feature of the nineteenth century.

THE CASTLE AND OLD TOWN WITH THE NEW TOWN BEYOND

Edinburgh Castle is seen here perched on a volcanic stub of rock which is precipitous on all but one side. The 'tail' which projects eastwards is a mound of earth and gravel created by the effects of glaciation and it was on this defensible site that the Old Town was built. The scouring effect of the glaciers also made a valley to the north of the ridge, which once contained a loch (the Nor' Loch) but is now a large open garden, normally green, in the centre of the city. Beyond, on a relatively flat area, can be seen the regular grid-iron pattern of Craig's New Town, with its two squares, one at either end. In the distance, the more irregular forms of the nineteenth-century extensions to the New Town can just be discerned.

THE HIGH STREET OF EDINBURGH

The High Street of Edinburgh, which is situated on the steep-sided narrow ridge running from the Castle Rock to Holyroodhouse, was one of the great streets of Medieval Europe; it was wide and straight and it was full of life. As Professor A.J. Youngson has said in The Making of Classical Edinburgh, *'Trade, shopping, gossip, fashion and business had for centuries been the life of the High Street . . . it was not only a public thoroughfare from the Castle to the Canongate, it was also a theatre of civic life.'*

The illustrations show the Lawnmarket and a section near to St Giles Cathedral; something of the medieval character of the place can be discerned even in these present-day views.

By the beginning of the eighteenth century little open space was left in the Old Town, which was by then a very crowded place. Tall buildings called 'lands' stood squashed together on the narrow building plots and these were occupied by all classes of society. The poorest would live on the lowest floors, where the smell from the refuse-laden street was greatest, and at the highest levels, which were the most inconvenient. The middle floors would be occupied by the better-off, including in many cases the owner of the property. Most of the medieval buildings in the Old Town were swept away in the nineteenth century but usually the pattern of streets and 'closes' (narrow alleys between the buildings) was retained.

58

GEORGE SQUARE

George Square, described by Professor A.J. Youngson in The Making of Classical Edinburgh as the first truly modern house-building project in Edinburgh and the first true square, was laid out in 1766 and was the most ambitious of the piecemeal developments which occurred in the late eighteenth century in response to overcrowding in the Old Town.

Of the original buildings, only the west side and a fragment of the east now remain. This is wholesome, unpretentious Georgian town architecture, mostly of rubble masonry set off by classical doorpieces. George Square is now at the heart of academic Edinburgh; the University's Faculties of Arts, Social Sciences and Medicine are all represented here, in rather pretentious Modernist architecture of reinforced concrete faced with a thin veneer of stone cladding.

REGISTER HOUSE AND THE NORTH BRIDGE

This view centres on one of Edinburgh's finest public buildings, Register House, which is situated at the east end of the New Town facing the line of the North Bridge. Both building and bridge resulted from initiatives taken in the late eighteenth century. The North Bridge was the link between the Old and New Towns and its construction was a vital part of the town council's plan to develop the land to the north of the burgh. The original structure, a masonry bridge of three arches, was opened for traffic in 1772 and was replaced by the present steel spans at the beginning of this century.

The erection of a suitable building to house the Public Records of Scotland was discussed at various times during the eighteenth century and funds finally became available in 1765. The building was designed by James and Robert Adam and is reminiscent of the Burlington-Kent school of English Palladianism. The dome and the delicately refined and restrained ornamentation derive, however, unmistakeably from the Adam office.

THE NORTH BRIDGE

The depth of the valley which separates the Old and New Towns can be judged from this view of the south end of the modern bridge. The High Street is seen on the left. Most of the buildings here date from the turn of the nineteenth and twentieth centuries, when the North Bridge was reconstructed, but an exception is the Tron Kirk, at the junction of the High Street and North Bridge. This was built in 1636-47 and is a good example of a T-plan Scottish post-Renaissance kirk.

THE SOUTH BRIDGE

The South Bridge, which runs southwards from the High Street on the extended line of the North Bridge, was a logical extension to the town's network of communications and made the first convenient connection between the Old Town and the land to the south of the Burgh. Built in 1785-88 by Robert Kay, it is a viaduct of nineteen arches, all but one of which are concealed by flanking buildings. These have a unified front, also by Kay, and possess some architectural pretension as is demonstrated by the presence of the several pediments which are clearly visible in the photograph. Robert Adam's Old College, completed by William Playfair, and now one of Edinburgh University's most treasured buildings, is seen on the extreme left.

CRAIG'S NEW TOWN FROM THE WEST

Craig's New Town of Edinburgh dates from 1767 and the plan is very much of its time, the rectilinear forms and strict geometric symmetry being appropriate for the neo-classical age – the Age of Enlightenment – in which rational thinking was considered superior to intuition. Humans are, of course, anything but logical and the most prominent sites in the plan – on the main axis and facing each other from the extremities of the two squares – were allocated for two city churches, whose activities are surely not connected with the rational mind. Both were built, but only St George's, in Charlotte Square and seen in the foreground here, occupies its intended site. It is now part of the Scottish Record Office.

CRAIG'S NEW TOWN – GEORGE STREET AND ST ANDREW SQUARE

Above right
At the very top of this picture, on the axis of George Street, may be seen the house of Sir Lawrence Dundas. It occupies the site in St Andrew Square which was intended for St Andrew's Church and which was acquired by its first owner, who has been described as a man of 'wealth and enterprise', in one of the most audacious 'shady' property deals to occur in Edinburgh.

Designed by Sir William Chambers in 1771, the house was considered to be one of the finest in the New Town. It has long been the headquarters of The Royal Bank of Scotland. Thus, instead of two churches facing each other along George Street, Edinburgh now

has records at one end and money at the other, which is no doubt appropriate in the twentieth century.

St Andrew's Church was eventually built, on a less prominent site in George Street, and is the building with the oval plan and tall spire seen in the middle-left of the photograph. It too is a fine piece of architecture, by Andrew Fraser, in the style of Wren and Gibbs.

CRAIG'S NEW TOWN BETWEEN FREDERICK STREET AND HANOVER STREET

Below left
In Craig's plan the rectilinear grid of principal streets formed a series of rectangular blocks of terraced houses which were bisected by secondary streets for artisans' houses, and these in turn were linked to a tertiary system of lanes for coach-houses. The layout was spacious and drying greens were provided between the rows of buildings. Commercial pressures in the nineteenth and twentieth centuries resulted in demolition of many of the original houses and of their replacement with shops and offices. At the same time most of the open space was built up.

The pattern of the original arrangement can still just be discerned in this view, however, especially in the block between George Street and Queen Street in the centre of the picture. Even in Princes Street, at the bottom of the picture, some of the original houses remain near the junctions with the transverse streets and it is just possible to imagine what the original residential street must have been like.

63

THE EAST END OF CRAIG'S NEW TOWN – ST ANDREW SQUARE

The building of the New Town was begun in the 1770s at the east end with St Andrew Square. The north side of this, where some of the original houses remain, is the best preserved and, although all of the buildings have been altered, the character of the original architecture can be judged. Similar to that of George Square, it is almost vernacular in its simplicity, with ornamentation confined to classical doorcases, although the rubble walls were originally faced with stucco.

One of Edinburgh's most famous landmarks, the Scott Monument, completed in 1846 as a memorial to Sir Walter Scott, one of Scotland's best-known and most influential writers, is seen in the lower left of this view.

THE WEST END OF CRAIG'S NEW TOWN – CHARLOTTE SQUARE
Charlotte Square was the final part of Craig's New Town to be built. Its grand manner is in complete contrast to the almost rustic simplicity of St Andrew Square and gives an indication of the extent to which architectural taste changed in Edinburgh in the last three decades of the eighteenth century. The north side, at the top here, consists of a row of eleven houses designed in 1791 with a 'palace-front' planned elevation in a single unified scheme. The architect was Robert Adam.

THE SECOND NEW TOWN

Queen Street Gardens, the horizontal strip of greenery in this view, separates the first New Town from the second, which was laid out by Robert Reid and William Sibbald in 1801-2. Heriot Row, facing the gardens and now one of Edinburgh's most exclusive streets, is similar to the latest parts of Craig's New Town. It is a well-mannered Georgian terrace on which an attempt has been made to impose a unified frontage, but, in true Edinburgh fashion, the respectability is somewhat superficial and the idiosyncrasies of the individual houses show up even in this aerial view. Beyond the plume of smoke caused by burning autumn leaves in Queen Street Gardens, the camera's eye picks up the curved forms of Royal Circus and the dramatic vista down Howe Street to Playfair's massive St Stephen's Church. These signify that the reason of neo-classicism is giving way to the Romanticism of the Picturesque.

66

IV

EDINBURGH IN THE
EARLY NINETEENTH
CENTURY

BY THE END of the 1790s the first New Town of Edinburgh was almost complete but even before it was finished plans were being made for its extension and building work continued almost without a break. The extended New Town is, however, an identifiable unit, the major part of which was built between 1802 and the early 1830s, and it may be treated as a discrete part of the city's development.

The 'Second New Town' was begun in 1802 on the land north of Queen Street, extending from Royal Circus in the west to London Street in the east. This was quickly followed by a 'Third', built around Calton Hill, and then a 'Fourth' on the Moray Estate between Charlotte Square and the Water of Leith. From 1817 onwards building was also taking place on the Raeburn Estate, adjacent to Stockbridge on the north bank of the Water of Leith, with the result that between 1802 and around 1830 the city, which had already doubled in area in the second half of the eighteenth century, doubled yet again.

The character of these new developments differed from that of Craig's original neo-classical New Town. Architectural fashion had changed and the Romantic idea of 'picturesqueness' was now in vogue. This originated in landscape-gardening, in which it took the form of deliberate attempts to create combinations of parks and buildings which recalled the landscape-paintings of such artists as Claude Lorrain and Gaspard Poussin. The notion of there being a 'spirit of place', which it was the duty of the landscape architect to elucidate and reinforce by interfering as little as possible with the natural contours and character of a site, was quickly added. The 'picturesque vista', terminated by a suitable building or monument, was a device which was also frequently used.

The extensions to the New Town of Edinburgh were planned in the spirit of the Picturesque. Instead of the 'rational' grid-iron plan of symmetrically disposed straight streets and squares of the first New Town, the second wave of building was an affair of crescents and irregular circuses – Moray Place, Abercromby Place, Royal Circus – and of vistas which were 'closed' by prominent buildings as in the view northwards down St Vincent Street to St Stephen's Church, or that along Waterloo Place to the various monuments on Calton Hill. The entire arrangement of buildings around Calton Hill is in fact perhaps the most perfect demonstration anywhere of the principles of 'Picturesque' planning: Playfair's terraces placed halfway up; the crown of the hill left free of building and used to create a 'field of monuments'; the siting of the former Royal High School building designed in the Greek Revival Style; the proximity of the slightly sinister Calton Jail and the organisation of the approach to the hill across Waterloo Bridge – all of these features – were models of 'picturesqueness'.

It must be said, of course, that the underlying topography of Edinburgh was ideally suited to this Romantic approach. It would scarcely have been possible to invent an arrangement of hills and valleys, including an Old Town complete with castle, cathedral and palace, which would better have lent itself to extension and enhancement according to the principles of the Picturesque Movement. It is fortunate and indeed something of a wonder that the architects and builders of the day, together with the city officials and private landowners who instructed them, were for the most part equal to the task and were thus able to seize the opportunity with which they were presented to produce a city of outstanding contrived beauty.

Nor were Calton Hill and the extended New Town the only examples of decision-making crucial to the development of the character of the city. The issue of how to make a second connection between the Old and New Towns, west of the North Bridge, was a live one at this time and involved a debate concerning the placing of a new bridge – George IV Bridge – over the Cowgate and a new road – Johnstone Terrace – on the south side of the Castle Rock. The problem of how all these roads should approach and be connected to the Royal Mile was the focus of much argument and it was fortunate that the solution which was finally agreed upon was so successful. The second link between Old and New Towns was made at the 'Mound', halfway along Princes Street, and the roadway was carried directly across the Royal Mile between the High Street and the Lawnmarket to form a second route south on the new bridge over the Cowgate. The road skirting the south side of the Castle Rock was merged with the Royal Mile further west at the head of the Lawnmarket. Various alternatives to this arrangement were proposed. One could have joined the Mound to the High Street near St Giles Cathedral, at a different point from the new road south, and would have required traffic moving south from Princes Street to dog-leg up the High Street. Another would have had all three new roads meet at a single junction in the Lawnmarket. Had one of these arrangements been adopted we can only imagine with horror what irreversible damage might have been caused to the city by the traffic planners of the 1950s and 1960s in an attempt to alleviate the traffic congestion which would surely have resulted. It is fortunate that the city fathers of the early nineteenth century had such good eyes for town planning.

There were, of course, other aspects of city management which left much to be desired: Edinburgh was declared bankrupt in 1833 and its accounts were not surprisingly found to be in a deplorable condition. Trustees were appointed and, in the aftermath, the growth of the city slowed down because the Council could not afford to encourage new developments by building the necessary infrastructure. This situation, however, was no more than was happening in most other large burghs at the time; the need for local government reform was pressing and the matter was in fact addressed later in the century.

The first half of the nineteenth century was also the period in which many of Edinburgh's prominent buildings and structures were erected. The Head Office of the Bank of Scotland, the buildings on the

Mound, St John's Church at the West End of Princes Street, the University's Old College, the Scott Monument, Edinburgh Academy, Donaldson's School and the Dean Bridge, to name only some of the better-known, were all constructed at this time. It was the period during which the essential character of the centre of Edinburgh was formed.

DRUMMOND PLACE
Above
ROYAL CIRCUS
The Second New Town was by far the largest single scheme in the development of Georgian Edinburgh. Its centrepiece was a single grand street, Great King Street, running from east to west between the two open spaces of Royal Circus and Drummond Place. Royal Circus is in fact a pair of crescents separated by irregularly shaped gardens and crossed by a serpentine road, a combination of elements which formed an ingenious solution to the difficulties caused by the slope of the site. Drummond Place, on less demanding contours, is more conventional and more severe and provides a pleasing complement to its neighbour.

CALTON HILL AND WATERLOO PLACE FROM THE WEST
Above right

The thoroughfare running vertically through this picture is Princes Street in the lower half with its extension of Waterloo Place in the upper half. The latter in fact runs on top of a bridge across the deep ravine which separates Calton Hill from the east end of Craig's New Town. It was designed by Robert Stevenson and Archibald Elliot and was built in response to the desires of the town council and Magistrates both to improve access to the east end of the New Town and to encourage further development of the city in the direction of Calton Hill. Waterloo Place was begun in 1816 at the same time as the street of the same name in London by John Nash. The buildings were designed to act as a frame for the view of Calton Hill from the east end of Princes Street, an idea which was clearly inspired by the Picturesque Movement.

CALTON HILL TERRACES FROM THE EAST
Below right

The scheme to develop the area around Calton Hill was initiated by four landowners, including the town council, who invited architects to submit plans for a suitable layout of streets and buildings. Thirty-two sets of plans were received, all of which advocated imposing formal patterns of streets on the irregular outline of the hill. They were condemned by the architect William Stark, who suggested that any building works on this

particular site should be sympathetic to the natural contours of the hill and that the architecture should be combined with foliage. In response to this view, William Playfair proposed the scheme which was eventually built, with two terraces halfway up the hill and the top left free for planting. It is a model of 'picturesqueness'. The scheme was not a financial success, however, because by the time that feuing started here, the western part of the city had become the fashionable area in which to live.

SYMBOLS, CALTON HILL

It was Robert Louis Stevenson who described the summit of Calton Hill as a 'field of monuments'. On the extreme left here is the old City Observatory by William Playfair (1818) who also designed the boundary wall containing, in the south-east corner, the small monument to his uncle John Playfair, who was President of the Astronomical Institution for which the observatory was built. The City Dome, in the north-east corner, was a later

addition (1895) by Robert Morham. In the centre of the picture is the Nelson Monument (1807), in the shape of a telescope, by William Burn. Clearly visible on the top of this are the cross-trees and the ball which to this day is raised and lowered at one o' clock as a time signal (originally to allow ships anchored in the Forth to set their chronometers). Further to the right is a fragment of the National Monument, an unfinished Parthenon, which was to have been built in honour of the dead of the Napoleonic Wars. Designed by

C.R. Cockrell and William Playfair, this is known colloquially as 'Edinburgh's disgrace' because the city was unable to raise sufficient funds for its completion from public subscription.

These forms, which are traditionally associated in western society with 'rationalism' and the 'masculine' are seen juxtaposed with the incised, white symbols suggestive of ancient cultures and more 'feminine' values, made by the contemporary artist Kate Whiteford.

On the Calton Hill
the twelve pillars
of this failed Parthenon
    made more Greek by the cargo boat
    sailing between them
    on the cobwebby water of the Firth
should marry nicely with the Observatory
in the way complements do
    each observing the heavens
    in its different way.
Yet these pillars fit better
with the man sat scrunched between them –
even his raincoat might have warded off the weather
all the way from Thebes. The scrip by his side
is filled with Scotch olives.

The illumination of new problems
burns on the tiderace that headlongs
straight as Princes Street
from dawn to dusk – as the sideslipping sun
makes flares of the windows of the North British Hotel
    they'll die back through blankness into windows
    and prove, tomorrow, illuminations
    are not answers.

And the man between the pillars
will be replaced by another
making through the windings of the world
towards his Ithaca and proving
there's no end to the windings
or the journeyings.

from INWARD BOUND

74

THE ROYAL HIGH SCHOOL

Conceived as a 'propylaeum' (a gateway of architectural importance) to the 'Acropolis' on which the ill-fated National Monument stands, and described by the distinguished architectural historian Sir John Summerson as '. . . the noblest monument of the Greek Revival . . .', the Royal High School is a building of international stature. It was constructed in 1825-29 to a design by Thomas Hamilton who maximised the potential of the very awkward site.

In 1977-78 it was converted to serve as the home of the proposed Scottish Assembly but has never been used for this purpose despite increasing dissatisfaction of the people of Scotland, expressed through the ballot box, with the politics which emanate from Westminster.

THE MOUND

Three of Edinburgh's most prominent buildings are visible here, the Royal Scottish Academy, the National Gallery of Scotland and the Head Office of the Bank of Scotland. The two galleries date from the early nineteenth century and were designed by William Playfair; the Royal Scottish Academy on the left is in the pure Greek Revival style while the National Gallery is more neo-classical in appearance. The Bank of Scotland was begun in 1802 but was enlarged in 1863 by David Bryce who must take the credit for its Baroque exterior.

The two galleries are situated on the Mound, which is the earthen causeway lying in the valley between the Old and New Towns and which was reputedly the result of the dumping of two million cartloads of earth and rubbish from the building of the New Town. It formed the obvious site for a road to link the two parts of the city and all three buildings mentioned above influenced the precise line which this eventually took. Three different routes for the road were projected. All shared the same stretch past the galleries. One would then have continued this straight line until it reached the top of the Royal Mile, at which point a large junction would have occurred with the two other new roads from the south and from the south-west. Another would have contained a right-angled bend near the end of the National Gallery and would have passed north of the Bank building before turning sharply southwards to join the High Street near

St Giles Cathedral, just visible in the top of the picture. Yet another, the route actually adopted, passed to the south of the Bank and joined the High Street at the foot of the Lawnmarket.

THE LAWNMARKET AND THE TOP OF THE MOUND
Below right
The points at which all three of the new roads mentioned previously join the Royal Mile can be seen in this photograph. The route up the Mound is visible in the bottom of the picture, where it curves eastward to pass south of the Bank of Scotland before turning sharply to join the High Street. George IV Bridge is seen joining the High Street from the south at the same point and Johnston Terrace, the route from the south-west, can just be seen entering the Lawnmarket further to the right. The Royal Mile itself is difficult to pick up in this view but runs more or less horizontally through the centre of the picture.

The medieval character of the buildings in the Lawnmarket is clearly shown, although most actually date from the nineteenth century. Also of interest is New College, in the lower middle of the photograph, which was built on the site of the palace of Mary of Guise, the mother of Mary, Queen of Scots. Originally the Free Church College and Assembly and now the Faculty of Divinity of Edinburgh University, it was constructed in 1846-50 by Playfair in a Tudor Collegiate style which contrasts with the classicism of the galleries lower down the Mound by the same architect.

ST GILES CATHEDRAL AND PARLIAMENT SQUARE

The buildings here seem to float in a sea of shadow, as well they might, because the figure of history has more than once chosen to make this the place where he conducts his melancholy business. The most prominent building is St Giles Cathedral, more correctly termed the High Kirk of Edinburgh, because it was in reality a cathedral for only two short periods in the seventeenth century when Stuart kings attempted to impose episcopacy on Scotland. The building dates from the twelfth century, but apart from the crown spire which is fifteenth-century and Robert Lorimer's Thistle Chapel of 1909-10 (the small appendage seen on the extreme right of the building), the exterior is almost entirely the result of a rebuilding which was carried out in 1829-33 under the direction of William Burn. Throughout its existence the church has played an important part in the life of the city. One of the most significant events which occurred there was the riot against episcopacy of 1637, said to have begun when a cabbage seller named Jenny Geddes threw a stool at the Dean as he attempted to read from the new service-book, and which was part of the upheaval which led to the signing of the National Covenant and eventually to the secure establishment of Presbyterianism in Scotland.

The High Street runs past one side of St Giles and on the other is Parliament Square, remodelled in 1807-10 by Robert Reid and so called because it was once the site of the Scottish Parliament. The Old Parliament Hall still exists – its medieval windows can just be seen in the lower right of the picture – and is now at the centre of 'legal' Edinburgh, because this complex of buildings houses the Writers to the Signet, the principal body of solicitors in Scotland, as well as the Court of Session and the High Court of Justiciary (not all visible in this view).

On the opposite side of the High Street is the City Chambers, built as a merchant exchange in 1754-61 to a design by John Adam, and now the home of Edinburgh District Council. This was one of the first substantial post-medieval buildings in the High Street and many older buildings were demolished to accommodate it. One sixteenth-century street – Mary King's Close – was not removed but simply built into the basement. It remains, substantially intact, to this day, complete with former houses and shops, Edinburgh's last medieval street.

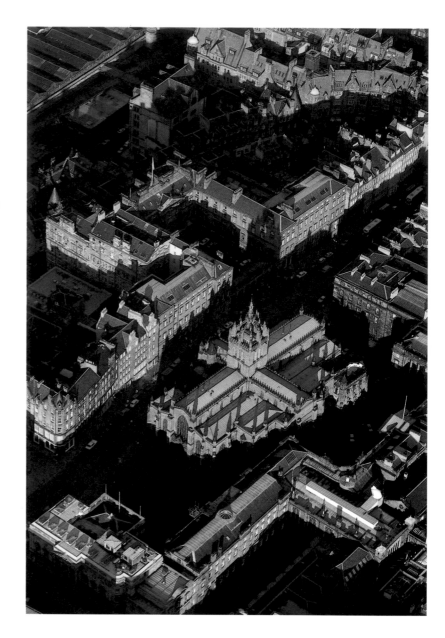

THE MORAY ESTATE
*James Gillespie Graham,
who planned the Moray
Estate development, was
conscious of the need for
imaginative design so as
to attract feuars who
might otherwise favour
Playfair's scheme at
Calton Hill. This was
especially important in
view of the precautions
which Lord Moray took
against financial liability;
the feuars here paid for
everything from houses to
streets, sewers, boundary
walls and Pleasure
Grounds. The
development was a
success nevertheless and
shifted the centre of
gravity of fashionable
Edinburgh westwards
away from the ill-fated
Calton scheme. Graham's
plan produced a
magnificent townscape
consisting of a crescent, an
oval and a polygon,
ingeniously linked to the
First and Second New
Towns. The complex
terrace which runs along
the north side of all three
spaces is said to be the
longest continuous row of
houses with a unified
front in Europe.*

THE MORAY ESTATE – MORAY PLACE

'It is, in the way of private building, the most splendid thing in Edinburgh.' So wrote Youngson of Moray Place in The Making of Classical Edinburgh.

THE MORAY ESTATE – AINSLIE PLACE AND THE PLEASURE GROUNDS

A feature of the Moray Estate development was the 'Pleasure Grounds', an area of landscaped garden on the steeply sloping ravine of the Water of Leith, at the northern boundary of the site. This was reserved for the exclusive use of the Moray feuars and was directly accessible from the back gardens of the adjacent houses, whose cliff-like forms are well displayed in this view.

THE DEAN BRIDGE AND DEAN VILLAGE

The Water of Leith runs more or less vertically through this picture. The Moray Estate, with its wooded Pleasure Grounds, is seen near the top, above the Dean Bridge, which was built in 1829-31, to a design by Thomas Telford. Lower still is the Dean Village, once bustling with meal mills, woollen mills and tanneries and now a quiet residential community which still preserves some of the character of a rural hamlet. In the 1880s Robert Louis Stevenson wrote of this scene: 'Over this [bridge], every afternoon, private carriages go spinning by, and ladies with card-cases pass to and fro about the duties of society. And yet down below you may still see, with its mills and foaming weir, the little rural village of Dean . . . [where] . . . the dusty miller comes to his door, looks out at the gurgling water, hearkens to the turning wheel and the birds about the shed, and perhaps whistles an air of his own to enrich the symphony.'

THE WATER OF LEITH – ST BERNARD'S WELL

Main picture opposite
The wooded banks of the ravine in which the Water of Leith passes through the New Town are mostly accessible only to local residents, but there is a public path, close to the river itself, linking the Dean Village to Stockbridge. This is a sheltered, mossy place appreciated by Edinburgh citizens who wish to take constitutionals on blustery Sunday afternoons, and there is even a watering place, in the guise of a circular Roman temple,
which is just visible in the photograph. This is St Bernard's Well, built over a mineral spring in 1789 and complete with pump room and a statue of Hygeia. It is still open to the public on certain Sundays, although the water is now deemed unsafe to drink.

THE RAEBURN ESTATE

Below right
The Raeburn Estate is so named because it was owned and developed by Sir Henry Raeburn, Scotland's greatest portrait painter, who is famed for the unrivalled pictorial record which he left of the principal figures of the Scottish Enlightenment. It lies opposite the Moray Estate on a bank of the Water of Leith, visible on the extreme right, and was developed from 1814 to designs by James Milne. It contains what is now arguably Edinburgh's most fashionable street, Ann Street, the most prominent of the rows of houses in the photograph. The buildings here are smaller in scale than in other parts of the New Town, which makes the street quaint as well as picturesque, and a somewhat rural quality is derived from the fact that there are front gardens, a very unusual feature for the time.

THE SCOTTISH NATIONAL GALLERY OF MODERN ART

This building was built in the 1820s, as John Watson's School, to the designs of William Burn. Since 1984 it has been the home of the Scottish National Gallery of Modern Art. The photograph depicts the rear of the building and shows to good effect the terrace of the gallery cafeteria, well-known for its fine fare and for its clientele, which is mostly upwardly mobile, if not predominantly young.

BOTANIC GARDENS

The keeper with a hating face
Skulks among the rosebushes
Whose useless flowers get on with their
Three weeks' explosion in the air.
His eyes, mad as a miser, glance
Through their unchilled extravagance.

Dangling from Pakistan, a blue
Flower reaches down into Peru;
A woman sits rocking a pram
Under the shadow of Assam;
From Norway two blue pigeons plane
To France; and China snows on Spain.

But in this Eden let two kiss –
The seraph in the trellises
Will drive them from the gates and stand,
A flaming by-law in his hand,
Directing their slow steps out of
This coloured no-man's-land of love.

For there's no season here to show
The way that any winds blow.
Frost and sun lie in one bed.
Winter-famished, summer-fed,
The naked and the clothed reveal
The contradictions of the real.

And time in more than one disguise
Jolts the cool logic of our eyes,
And man's intrusion proves that he
Is madder, only, than this tree
Which spends its virtue to contrive
That snow on fire should be alive.

THE ROYAL BOTANIC GARDEN, EDINBURGH

The botanic garden produces patterns of foliage quite unlike those found in the countryside because each tree or shrub in it is different from its neighbour. Edinburgh's Garden originated as a physic garden which was first established in the vicinity of Holyrood Abbey around 1670 by two Edinburgh physicians, Robert Sibbald and Robert Balfour. Its purpose was to provide plants and herbs for medicinal use and it seems to have undergone continuous expansion from the day of its beginning. A second garden was opened at Trinity Hospital (Waverley Station now stands on the site) in 1676 and the two were amalgamated and moved to a larger site in Leith Walk in 1763. Soon, this also became too small and the move to the present location at Inverleith was made around 1824. Since this time the Garden has continued to expand, mainly as a consequence of systematic collecting of plants by its staff during expeditions the world over. The collection of rhododendrons is particularly fine and is the largest in Britain. The Royal Botanic Garden at Edinburgh is now an important centre for taxonomic research, especially on the plants of China and the Himalayas.

The Royal Botanic Garden, in spring, summer, autumn and (overleaf) winter.

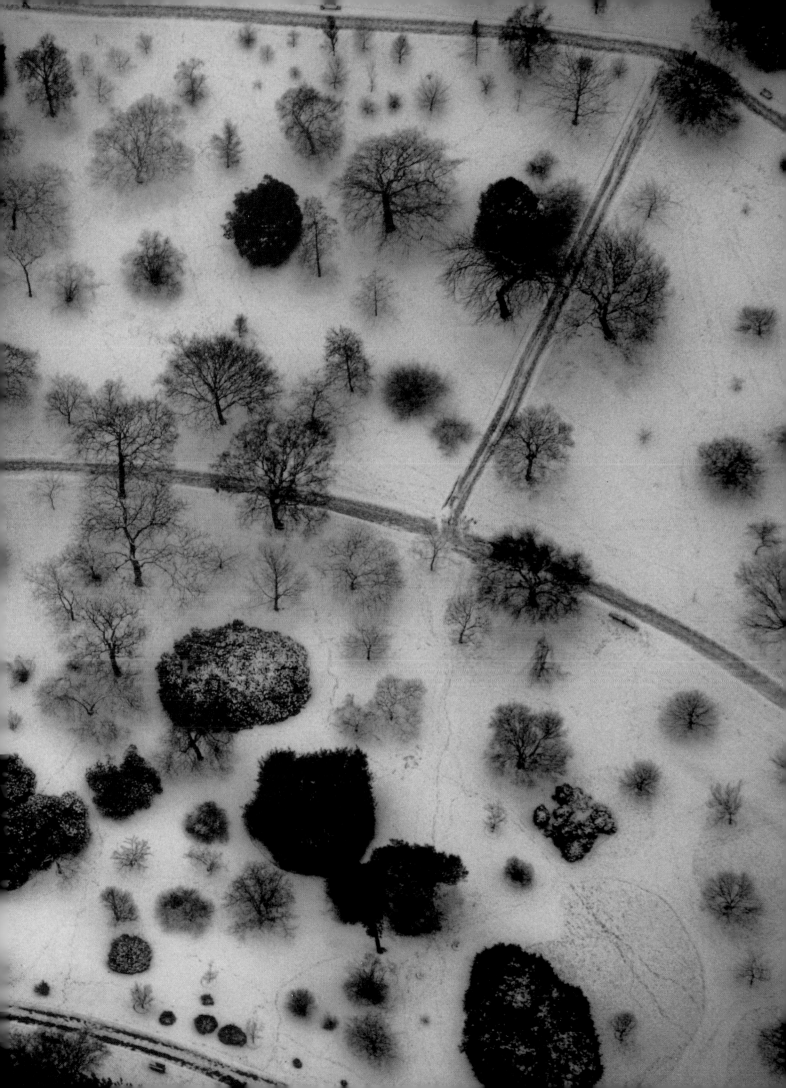

CHAMBERS STREET, OLD COLLEGE AND THE ROYAL MUSEUM OF SCOTLAND

The area of Edinburgh shown here changed out of recognition in the nineteenth century. The building in the foreground is Old College of Edinburgh University, considered by many to be Robert Adam's greatest public work, although only the exterior is actually by Adam. Construction of this began in 1789 but was halted in 1793, following the outbreak of the Napoleonic Wars, and did not resume until 1819, by which time William Playfair, who was responsible for the elevations to the quadrangle and all of the interiors, was in charge. It was his first commission and he gave such a good account of himself that he was immediately flooded with work and thus established in his career as a leading Edinburgh architect. Playfair's work here was finished in 1837 and the dome was added by R. Rowand Anderson in 1879.

The large building in the centre of the picture is now the Royal Museum of Scotland, Chambers Street, part of the National Museums of Scotland, and dates from 1861. It has a memorable main hall – an interior of iron and glass reminiscent of the Crystal Palace in London, of which it was a near contemporary. The designer was the engineer Francis Ffowke.

Chambers Street itself was not created in its present form until 1867 when three eighteenth-century squares were demolished to make this connection between the two principal routes south from the Old Town, South Bridge (bottom of the picture) and George IV Bridge (top).

Two other historic buildings, Greyfriars Church and Heriot's Hospital (now George Heriot's School), can be seen at the top of the photograph.

DONALDSON'S SCHOOL

Donaldson's is now a school for the deaf but was originally endowed as an orphan hospital by James Donaldson. It is by William Playfair and is in the style of English Tudor courtyard houses such as Burghley and Audley End; it demonstrated the architect's versatility, as well as his perseverance. It was his most protracted commission, stretching from 1841 until its completion in 1854, and apparently almost drove him into retirement; he is reputed to have said: 'Better freedom and porridge and milk than slavery with venison and claret.' The building had the dubious privilege of being bombed by a Zeppelin in 1916.

The very last part of Edinburgh's New Town, the somewhat formidable western crescents, constructed in the 1870s, are seen at the top of this photograph.

ST MARY'S (EPISCOPAL) CATHEDRAL, EDINBURGH

St Mary's Cathedral – built in 1874-1917 – dominates Edinburgh's western New Town, which is perhaps appropriate as it was the proprietors of the surrounding buildings who paid for its construction, albeit indirectly. The Misses Walker, heirs of Sir Patrick Walker on whose land this part of the city was developed, left their fortune to the Episcopal Church on condition that it be used to build a cathedral for the diocese of Edinburgh on this site. The twin spires at the western end of the building are accordingly named Barbara and Mary in their memory. G. Gilbert Scott was the architect.

FETTES COLLEGE

Fettes College is one of a number of independent schools within the boundaries of Edinburgh and its main building is the city's most formidable 'Victorian pile'. Endowed by Sir William Fettes, a former Lord Provost of the city, it was built in 1864-70 in a style which is an amalgam of Scottish Baronial and French Gothic. The architect was David Bryce.

89

Kamikaze swifts dive-bomb the rooftops
(missing them every time) then soar
screaming and wheeling –
if they towed pencils behind them
they'd draw huge baskets in the sky.

. . .

In the evening villages
men are sucked into pubs
to talk like ruminants
and drink like stirrup-pumps.

And the corn grows
gluttonously towards fruition,
towards the day when the combine harvester
clanks from a nightmare mind
and lurches into the field.

And all the uprising forces
will dwindle and die down,
leaving it to the sleeping earth
to dream them up again.

from SEASONAL NOTES – JUNE

V

THE LANDSCAPE IN THE EIGHTEENTH AND NINETEENTH CENTURIES

THE PATTERN of the present-day landscape of southern Scotland was mainly created during the eighteenth century in the age of agricultural 'improvement'. It is made up of flat fields enclosed by hedges, dykes and shelter belts – the landscape of agriculture – and parklands of grass and trees, these being associated with large country houses. Most of what is visible is almost entirely artificial and is a thin, somewhat precarious, veneer of cultivation lying either on 'raised beaches' near the coasts of Fife and East Lothian, or on gently undulating boulder clay soil, on the higher ground of both Fife and the Lothians. It is punctuated by steep-sided volcanic remnants, such as Traprain Law, and outcrops of whin-covered rocks, which serve as reminders of more fundamental shapers of the landscape, such as the ice sheets of the last ice age, and of the deeper geology of mainly sedimentary and volcanic rock.

All of this land was forested originally but most of the trees had been removed by the Middle Ages. The agricultural landscape of the medieval period was very different from that of today, however; there were few trees and the fields were very much larger than they are now, and were subdivided into strips by a ridge and furrow system which was necessary to allow surface drainage to occur effectively. This was also a convenient arrangement for working the land with hand tools. In feudal times the bulk of the population lived in the countryside and individuals were granted the right to cultivate a few strips of land, selected usually from widely separated parts of the very large fields in order that each would have a share of the best and the worst land. This was subsistence farming. There were few farmhouses as such and the population lived mainly in clusters of peasants' houses ('farmtouns').

By the sixteenth century, feudal tenure had almost disappeared in South-East Scotland and most estates were subdivided into small farms, each with a tenant farmer living in a farmhouse and employing field workers, who lived either in farm bothies or in rows of cottages adjoining the farm. The strip system of cultivation was still in use, however, and the only areas of usable land not divided into ridges and furrows were the common grazings and the parklands which surrounded the large country houses. These must have stood out amongst the treeless tracts of landscape as if to emphasise the dominance of the whole system by the landowner.

This medieval pattern of landscape was swept away by the agricultural revolution of the eighteenth century and early nineteenth century and very little of it remains today. Traces of the ridge and furrow system can however be seen on the Lammermuir Hills, in the marginal uplands where cultivation was abandoned during the 'improvement' period. Another fairly obvious survival is on what is now

Prestonfield Golf Course in Edinburgh. Over most of the countryside the large fields were levelled – something which was feasible only after the development of techniques of underground drainage – and sub-divided into the relatively small fields which we see today. The simultaneous introduction of farm machinery, the use of which was now possible in the level fields and which had in fact been used in the levelling, contributed to a reduced requirement for agricultural labour and many workers joined the growing tide of migrants to the towns. Some stayed on in the countryside, living now in villages, which were another feature of the new landscape, and finding employment either on the land or in the new rural industries associated with farm machinery or crop processing which had sprung up around the 'improved' agriculture. Farming was now a commercial enterprise – a business rather than a means of subsistence – and on the fertile lands of South-East Scotland it became increasingly profitable. The many fine farmhouses and steadings which date from the immediate post-improvement period testify to this.

There was, of course, another side to the 'improvement' coin, which was the virtual disappearance of small and relatively independent peasant farmers many of whom had no choice but to become farm labourers on larger farms, following the restructuring of agriculture during the 'improvement' period. The new appearance of the country-side symbolised for some the nature of the recast rural community and the lack of justice inherent in the new system by which land was worked.

Set within the agricultural landscape, the parklands which surround-ed the country houses – the seats of the landowners – were still present. As the photographs show, many of the houses themselves are now somewhat dilapidated and are probably destined to become either museums or piles of stones, like the feudal castles which they succeeded – reminders of bygone social structures. In the eighteenth century they were in their heyday and it was here that the arts of architecture and of landscape gardening were practised in the countryside.

The building of large country houses in Scotland was heavily influenced by trends south of the Border, but at the beginning of the eighteenth century, under the dominating figure of William Adam (father of Robert, James and John), it nevertheless retained a definite Scottish character. Mavisbank, for example, which was the product of a collaboration between Adam and its owner, while owing much to Palladio and Vanburgh, exhibits a typical Scottish verticality of manner. The later Penicuik House is cloned directly from English Palladianism, however, while Gosford, by Robert Adam, and dating from the end of the century, is truly international. Seton Castle, also by Robert Adam, is an hybrid of Gothic and classical forms, and is of much interest as an example of the Romantic and Picturesque move-ments which affected both Scotland and England in the late eighteenth and early nineteenth centuries.

Landscape architecture in Scotland remained more individual and distinctively Scottish than its counterpart in built form, perhaps because it was more dependent on the vagaries of the local terrain and climate. In the late seventeenth century the formal garden was fashionable, and that at Kinross House (now much altered) was an example. The eighteenth century was the period when Lancelot ('Capability') Brown was creating his 'ideal', somewhat manicured, 'landscapes' in England, and the influence of the English landscape tradition, in which a classical house is set within an informal landscaped park, can be seen at Mavisbank and at Penicuik. Formal gardens were still popular in Scotland, however, and eighteenth-century formal planting can be seen at Tyninghame and Hopetoun.

EVIDENCE OF RIDGE AND FURROW CULTIVATION

Each of these photographs shows traces of pre-improvement ridge-and-furrow cultivation systems, which have been long-abandoned and are now overlaid by the effects of more recent land-use activities. At Wanside, on the northern fringe of the Lammermuir Hills, the irregularly shaped mounds near the bottom of the picture are the remains of farmtoun buildings and these are surrounded by evidence of cultivation strips. More strips are present in the middle distance at the further side of a more recent square-shaped field. The drainage ditches at the extreme bottom edge of the picture are of very recent origin. Near Longformacus in Berwickshire, on the southern edge of the same range of hills, the long-since-abandoned cultivation strips are shown up particularly well by the light dusting of snow. A recently planted shelter belt is also evident in this picture. The fourth picture shows the Duddingston area of Edinburgh: Duddingston Village is in the foreground and Duddingston Loch in the middle distance. The snow-covered stretch of ground near the top of the photograph is Prestonfield Golf Course, on which traces of strip cultivation can be discerned.

WANSIDE,
EAST LOTHIAN
Above right
BLACK HILL,
BERWICKSHIRE
Below right

LONGFORMACUS,
BERWICKSHIRE
Above
DUDDINGSTON
AND
PRESTONFIELD,
EDINBURGH
Below

95

DUNBAR COMMON FROM DEUCHRIE EDGE, EAST LOTHIAN

The flattish ground in the upper half of this picture is Dunbar Common on the Lammermuir Hills. As its name suggests, this land would have been used for animal pasture in the medieval period, probably organised on the 'sheiling' system in which animals together with people to tend them went to this high ground during the summer months. The practice was at its height in the twelfth and thirteenth centuries in South-East Scotland under the jurisdiction of the monasteries and was used mainly for sheep husbanding in connection with the wool trade. In the late Middle Ages the Border monasteries exported large quantities of wool to the Low Countries. The tracks giving access to the higher ground, which are still used by sheep farmers today but which probably date from medieval times, are clearly seen in this picture.

The sheiling system died out when the old run-rig type of cultivation ended. Once the arable farmland was divided into individual farm units, with each farm having its own fields on which crop rotation was practised, and sown grasses being used in conjunction with better processing of hay, farms became reasonably self-sufficient and did not require the use of seasonal upland pasture. These hills are nevertheless still used for sheep grazing. A modern, well-ordered farm steading, dating from the 'improvement' period, is seen at the bottom of the picture.

96

OLD ROAD, LAMMERMUIR HILLS, EAST LOTHIAN

In medieval times the Lammermuirs were crossed by a number of roads which ran from Haddington and the coastal burghs to Lauderdale. They were used by all varieties of travellers and also for the transport of essential commodities; large quantities of salted herring passed southwards to the Borders along these routes; wool for export passed northwards to the ports. The roads were not deliberately made but were formed through repeated use by traffic. Where the going was firm everyone would use the same track but on steep slopes or where soft ground was encountered, each rider or carter would find his own route, with the result that these old roads tended to expand and contract in width depending on the nature of the terrain underfoot. This pattern is clearly seen in the picture here which depicts one of the old herring roads running south from Lothian Edge.

97

ENCLOSED FIELDS, SALTOUN, EAST LOTHIAN

The large building in the centre left of this picture is Saltoun Hall. Andrew Fletcher of Saltoun, who was born in 1653, was one of the early improvers (and, incidentally, a vigorous opponent of the Act of Union of 1707), but most of what is seen here today dates from the nineteenth century. The white, snow-covered roofs of the home farm are in the top-centre of the picture, surrounded by a pattern of enclosed fields. Level fields like these (i.e. fields not containing ridges and furrows) were only possible after the development of techniques of underground drainage. The essential piece of technology was the unglazed tile drain pipe and many estates built small factories to produce these, both for their own use and for sale to neighbouring farms. A brick and tile factory was set up on the Saltoun estate in 1834 and within a decade had produced half a million drainage tiles. Most of these would be used locally, which gives an indication of the rate at which field levelling was progressing at this time.

SHELTER BELT AND CAREFULLY TENDED LEVELLED FIELD, FIFE

FIELDS OF CORN AT BIEL HOUSE, EAST LOTHIAN

The levelled, enclosed fields of post-improvement agriculture show up well in this view in which fields of ripening grain are enclosed by shelter belts and hedges. A substantial number of farm steadings is visible, and the occasional green field of sown grass pasture indicates that crop rotation is being practised. Robert Burns, who possessed a tenant farmer's eye for the land, described East Lothian as, '. . . the most glorious corn country I ever saw.'

FARM BUILDINGS DATING FROM THE NINETEENTH CENTURY, EAST LOTHIAN

It was in 1699 that Lord Belhaven wrote his famous treatise on agricultural 'improvement' (The Country Man's Rudiments: or An Advice to the Farmers in East Lothian) *and outlined his ideas on the layout of farm buildings, and this led to the building of steadings to replace farmtouns in the eighteenth century. Most of the existing steadings in East Lothian date from the nineteenth century, however, when the increasing prosperity of farmers led to a second wave of building, and four of these are shown here. In all cases the farmhouse is separate from the steading itself, an indication of the increasing social distance between the farmer and his workers. The farmhouses of this period were substantial buildings, based, in their design, on rural manses or small laird's houses. All of the examples shown have slate roofs. This is typical, because slate was considered a superior roofing material to pantiles, which were normally reserved for the steadings. The steadings show a variety of plan-forms; all would originally have consisted of a group of barns, byres and stables arranged around a courtyard – this was the archetypal layout proposed by Lord Belhaven – though subsequent additions have in all cases here reduced the size of the original courtyard. Three of the steadings have chimneys, indicating that they once housed steam-*

LUGGATE
Above
GARVALD GRANGE
Below right

driven threshing machines, and sharp eyes will detect the polygonal roof-form of a horse gin in the top left corner of the Garvald Grange steading which would have provided the power for threshing in this case. Papple is a fine example of a steading in which the original group of single-storey buildings with pantiled roofs has had a new range, containing an entrance gateway, added to it in the late nineteenth century. This takes the form of an architectural composition in the Gothic Revival style and is typical of the imposing additions made to aggrandise the more prosperous farms. At Luggate, a row of farm cottages is seen just beyond the trees surrounding the farmhouse. These would have been for married workers; unmarried male workers were usually housed collectively in single-room bothies built into the steading.

BARBERFIELD
Above
PAPPLE
Below left

101

PLANNED VILLAGES

Prior to the eighteenth century, villages were a rarity in Scotland; there was no reason for their existence because the system of agriculture was such that it was convenient for the rural population to live in farmtouns scattered through the countryside. The changing conditions of the age of 'improvement' created a need for nucleated settlements, however, and the resulting villages tended to have regular layouts because they were planned in a single operation. A 'planned village movement' began in Scotland in the first half of the eighteenth century; sometimes a village was created as a centre for marketing agricultural produce; another reason might be to establish rural industry, or the intention might be simply to bring the various activities of an estate together at one location. Both of the villages illustrated here date from the eighteenth century, although most of the existing buildings are of the nineteenth. Tyninghame is often referred to as a model 'estate village'. It has a factor's house, a sawmill, a baker's house, a schoolhouse, a widow's row and a smith's house, together with accommodation for estate workers, all brought together in a regular pattern with just sufficient variety to prevent monotony. There had in fact been a village at Tyninghame prior to the eighteenth century but this was demolished to accommodate alterations to the parkland surrounding the House. The same was true of Gavinton.

TYNINGHAME
Above
GAVINTON
Below right

BALCASKIE, FIFE

By the seventeeth century a distinctive type of garden plan had emerged in Scotland, consisting of a walled garden of limited extent, within which the various parts were arranged in an orderly manner. This was codified in The Scots Gardener of 1683, the author of which was John Reid, gardener to Sir George MacKenzie of Rosehaugh, and for whom 'the greatest calamity was irregularity'. Balcaskie House, which is in the East Neuk of Fife and faces south across the Firth of Forth, was remodelled in 1668-74 by Scotland's first truly classical architect, Sir William Bruce, for his own use. The existing house had an L-shaped plan and Bruce added to this to create a symmetrical arrangement with pavilions, reminiscent of the villas of Palladio. To the south of the house he constructed three terraces which, taken together, formed a large rectangular enclosure within which was laid out a garden which would no doubt have satisfied Reid. Beyond this walled garden the planting continued the axis of the house into the landscape and this line would, in fact, if projected, have passed through the Bass Rock, a prominent feature on the horizon 15 miles away off the East Lothian coast. This device of incorporating the naturally occurring features of the topography into designed landscapes was often used by Bruce and was an aspect of his work which anticipated the 'Picturesque Movement' of one hundred years later. The gardens at Balcaskie were much altered in both the nineteenth and the twentieth centuries, but the underlying structure of Bruce's design is nevertheless still the basis of the present arrangements.

MAVISBANK, MIDLOTHIAN

Financed by the profits from coal-mining and now a hopeless ruin as a consequence of twentieth-century neglect and, ironically, mining subsidence, Mavisbank is seen here set within its landscaped park and with the remains of its kitchen garden nearby. It was built in 1724-39 to the designs of its owner Sir John Clerk with the architect William Adam. The house is important as one of Scotland's early classical mansions but the landscaping is perhaps even more interesting as this was one of Scotland's very first 'informal' designed landscapes, in which a break was made with the tradition of regularity, such as is seen at Balcaskie, and a more 'natural' effect sought, albeit a somewhat contrived naturalism. Similar developments were occurring in England led by William Kent and later by Lancelot ('Capability') Brown but, though the English work would have been known to Clerk, who was very well travelled, he was no mere copyist but a man of original ideas who wrote extensively on the planning of country houses and their parks. In England the freedom in nature which was evoked by the new informal landscapes was given symbolic meaning and was associated with ideas of political freedom (the constitutional power struggle between Crown and Parliament was by no means over at this time). No such connections were made by Clerk, for whom the key to the landscape movement was emotional and literary rather than political.

PENICUIK HOUSE AND HURLEY POND, MIDLOTHIAN

Sir John Clerk, who built Mavisbank, was also the owner of the Penicuik estate where he created another informal park. Sir John was renowned for his ability to translate pastoral and poetical ideas into landscape. He planted 300,000 trees here between 1700 and 1730 and made the famous Hurley Ponds, one of which is seen in the photograph, and which he described as '. . . noteworthy for its position and solitude, which a poet only could describe'. Penicuik House, also in the photograph, was built in 1761-69 to a design by Sir John's son, Sir James Clerk, with assistance from a master mason called John Baxter. (The end wings were added later by David Bryce.) Like his father, Sir James was a competent amateur architect, and he produced what Colin McWilliam in the Lothian volume of The Buildings of Scotland *has described as 'the ideal of a Scottish Palladian house'. It was gutted by fire in 1899 and is now a dangerous ruin, and the subject of an appeal fund for its stabilisation.*

SETON HOUSE AND COLLEGIATE CHURCH, EAST LOTHIAN

Seton House occupies the site of the old palace of the Setons, who were granted the lands of Seton and Winton in the twelfth century, and who became one of the wealthiest and most influential families in Scotland. The palace was described as the most magnificent in Scotland – Mary, Queen of Scots,

James VI and Charles I were all entertained there – but it became ruinous in the eighteenth century following forfeiture of the estate after the family found itself on the losing side in the Jacobite rebellion of 1715. It was demolished in 1790 but its boundary walls still form the precinct of the new house. This was started in the same year and is one of Robert Adam's castle-style houses. It is remarkable for possessing a combination of classical and Gothic features. Like Culzean in Ayrshire, it shows Adam at his most Romantic and anticipates the Romanticism of the nineteenth century.

Seton Collegiate Church dates from the fifteenth century although there was a church here from the thirteenth century. The spire was never finished.

105

GOSFORD HOUSE, EAST LOTHIAN

Gosford House gives an indication of the prosperity of some of the landowners of South-East Scotland in the eighteenth and nineteenth centuries, when profits from coal-mines and farming were high. This house is one of the last which Robert Adam designed – the dome is an unmistakeable Adam touch – and one of the last large classical country houses to be built in Scotland. The central block only is by Adam and even this has a front which was altered from Adam's design – this part of the house was not completed until 1800, eight years after Adam's death. The two end pavilions are later work by the Glasgow architect William Young and were completed in 1891.

POND, GOSFORD
HOUSE,
EAST LOTHIAN

MAUSOLEUM,
GOSFORD HOUSE,
EAST LOTHIAN

107

'SCOTT'S VIEW' –
THE ROMANTIC
LANDSCAPE,
ETTRICK AND
LAUDERDALE

Both of these photographs were taken from approximately above the spot where Sir Walter Scott used to request his coachman to stop so that he could admire the view of the River Tweed and the Eildon Hills, with the ruined abbey of Melrose in the far distance. Scott was one of the literary romantics who changed national and international consciousness around the turn of the eighteenth century and paved the way for the Romantic Movement which was to dominate the architecture as well as all the other arts of the nineteenth century.

108

TYNINGHAME HOUSE, EAST LOTHIAN

Tyninghame has an interesting history dating back to the seventh century. The present house was the result of a remodelling of a seventeenth-century building which was carried out in 1829-30 under the architect William Burn. Its mullioned bay-windows, candle-snuffer roofs, bundles of chimneys and Jacobean flavour make it a fine example of the Scottish Baronial Revival, one strand of the Romantic Movement of the nineteenth century. The park at Tyninghame is a pioneer work of landscaping, mostly dating from the seventeenth century, but the formal gardens close to the house are contemporary with the remodelling of 1830 and indicate a revival of interest in older gardening practices which became fashionable in the nineteenth century.

The two arches at the bottom of the photograph are part of the ruined twelfth-century St Baldred's Church. The tree felling close to this occurred in 1988 when the house was subdivided into separate occupancies following its sale by the Earl of Haddington, whose family had been the proprietors here since 1628.

DROP-OUT IN EDINBURGH

I steal nothing from you.
I am your incandescent heir.
You bequeath me my incandescence.

City of everywhere, broken necklace in the sun,
you are caves of guilt, you are pinnacles of jubilation.
Your music is a filigree of drumming.
You frown into the advent of heavenly hosts.
Your iron finger shatters sad suns –
they multiply in scatters, they swarm
on fizzing roofs. When the sea
breathes gray over you, you become
one lurking-place, one shifting of nowheres –
in it are warpipes and genteel pianos
and the sawing voices of lawyers. Your buildings
are broken memories, your streets
lost hopes – but you shrug off time, you set your face
against all that is not you.

I am your incandescent heir.
I am your morning side, I am your golden acre.
Your windows glitter me, the sheen
on your pigeons' breasts is me.
I glide through your dark streets like phosphorus.

VI

THE NINETEENTH CENTURY – AN AGE OF INDUSTRY AND SOCIAL REFORM

THE FIRST Industrial Revolution did not touch the East of Scotland in the same way as it did the West, which was its heartland north of the Border. Fife and East Lothian remained predominantly rural in the nineteenth century, as did the Borders, and it was only really in West Lothian and in a ring around the fringes of Edinburgh above the Lothian Coalfield that the landscape became scarred by the activities of industry. This took the form mainly of 'bings' or spoil heaps produced by coal- and shale-mining because, although most of the activities which characterised the Industrial Revolution were present in South-East Scotland – iron and steel (foundries if not smelters), shipbuilding, engineering and textiles – manufacturing was altogether on a smaller scale than in the West. The fact that industries were present, however, led to the improvement of communications and the nineteenth century was a time of railway and canal building and of improvements to docks and harbours.

If the East did not have the same predominance of smoking chimneys and belching furnaces as the West, it did have its fair share of the social evils which went with early industrialisation. Poverty and squalor were the everyday realities of much of the urban working class, particularly in Edinburgh, and were a threat to the well-being of the whole population. They provided the stimulus for social and political reforms: the old systems of poor relief and education based on the Kirk and its parishes were inadequate to meet the needs of an industrialised society and the second half of the nineteenth century saw the gradual transfer of responsibility for these to secular authorities. Most of the important reforms were initiated by central government but the mechanisms by which they were carried through involved the setting up of elected local authorities or Boards, to minister to the various social needs of the population, funded out of rates on property. The reform of local government, which was long overdue, was therefore an essential part of this fight against social ills. The effects of these reforms can be seen on the landscape today: the Education (Scotland) Act of 1872, for example, led to the widespread building of 'Board Schools' in town and country alike in the closing decades of the century. Some of the great hospital buildings – the present Royal Infirmary of Edinburgh being an example – also date from this period, as do many programmes for building improved housing.

The Victorian Age was not concerned solely with industrial development and the amelioration of its darker consequences. It was also an age of enjoyable leisure for increasing numbers of people and the evidence for this too can be seen today. Seaside towns, especially those with a railway connection such as St Andrews or North Berwick, became resorts and flourished; golf became a popular pastime and golf courses were constructed in profusion. Many of those in South-East Scotland, such as Muirfield at Gullane and the 'Old Course' at St Andrews, were destined to become world-famous. Spectator sport on a large scale was another phenomenon which originated in its present form in the Victorian Age and edifices such as Tynecastle Football Stadium are a testament to this. This period, therefore, as all others, added its multicoloured threads to the rich tapestry of the landscape.

STOCKBRIDGE
'COLONIES',
EDINBURGH
*The Stockbridge
'Colonies' lie on the
northernmost fringe of
Edinburgh's New Town
on a bank of the Water of
Leith. These eleven
parallel streets of one-
and two-storey flatted
houses were constructed
in 1861-65 by the
Edinburgh Co-operative
Building Association to
provide low cost housing
for working people and
are the best known of
several 'colonies' within
the city. The Society was
founded by the Revd
James Begg, a Church of
Scotland minister and
author of* Happy Homes
for Working Men *who
was much concerned with
the appalling conditions
in which the poor of
Edinburgh were housed
in the nineteenth century,
particularly in the Old
Town. Although intended
for working-class owner-
occupiers, their
desirability led to their
passing quickly into the
ownership of the middle
class.*

TENEMENTS IN MARCHMONT, EDINBURGH

From the middle of the nineteenth century a large area of Edinburgh south of the Old Town was built up – the 'South Side'. The character of this area was somewhat different from that of either the Old Town, which in the nineteenth century was occupied by the 'unwashed', and the New Town, where the aristocracy and upper middle class lived. The South Side was created for the aspiring lower middle class. The photograph shows tenements in Marchmont, but similar buildings are to be found in Bruntsfield and Morningside. There is just a hint of Scottish Baronial in these solid, uniform and eminently respectable dwellings, which Colin McWilliam has described as, '. . . fortresses, comfortable within but anonymous without, into which the mass of Edinburgh's middle class abdicated from participation in the city's townscape'.

SOUTH SIDE – THE 'VILLA QUARTERS', EDINBURGH

In the southern part of the South Side, tenements give way to terraces, and semi-detached and detached houses, and the tone of the neighbourhood rises a few points on Edinburgh's well-defined social scale. The houses here are mainly the products of Victorian speculative builders and were designed for massiveness and showiness so as to be attractive to the rising professional class. The areas of the city thus created – Grange, Newington, Salisbury –

were described by Robert Louis Stevenson in his waspish commentary Picturesque Notes, written in 1878, as the 'villa quarters'. He reserved a special disdain for the quality of the architecture:
'They are not buildings; for you can scarcely say a thing is built when every measurement is in clamant disproportion with its neighbour. They belong to no style of art, only to a form of business much to be regretted. On the other hand, there is a noble way of being ugly: a high-aspiring fiasco like the fall of Lucifer . . . To aim at making a commonplace villa, and to make it insufferably ugly in each particular; to attempt the homeliest achievement and to attain the bottom of derided failure; not to have any theory but profit and yet, at an equal expense, to outstrip all competitors in the art of conceiving and rendering permanent deformity; and to do all this in what is, by nature, one of the most agreeable neighbourhoods in Britain: what are we to say, but that this also is a distinction, hard to earn, although not greatly worshipful?'

114

STENTON, EAST LOTHIAN

Stenton is a delightful village in East Lothian close to the Lammermuir Hills and is thought to be of medieval origin. It is not close to the sea, to the railway nor to any main road and must, in the nineteenth century, have been fairly remote. It has nevertheless been touched by the reforming movements of the latter part of the century, which were triggered by conditions in the industrial towns, because it boasts a Board School (lower left), built in 1878 as a direct result of the Education (Scotland) Act of 1872. This Act had a profound effect on the education system in Scotland, which, it must be pointed out, was already better than that which existed in most European countries, including England. It set up the Scotch (later Scottish) Education Department and made schooling compulsory for all between the ages of 5 and 13. It also transferred the responsibility for running schools from the Kirk to locally elected School Boards. It was one of a series of Acts passed in the late nineteenth century which reorganised the provisions made for education, poor relief, policing and other aspects of social welfare. By placing the responsibility for these in the hands of elected bodies empowered to raise revenue by taxes on property, the various Acts brought into being the system of democratically elected local authorities which has been an important aspect of government ever since.

McEWAN HALL AND BRISTO SQUARE, EDINBURGH

A graduation ceremony has just taken place in the University's McEwan Hall and graduands and doting parents are enjoying the sunshine and sharing Bristo Square with members of the skateboarding fraternity, who have been the principal beneficiaries of this most recent of Edinburgh's created public 'places'. The McEwan Hall was built in 1888-89 to a design by R. Rowand Anderson out of funds provided by a well-known Edinburgh brewer – an early act of sponsorship of the University. Also in the photograph are two student union buildings; the older Teviot Row Union (Sydney Mitchell & Wilson, 1888) is in the top left and the modern Student Centre (Morris & Steedman, 1966-73) fills the lower half of the picture. Many of the users of these facilities operate a reciprocal form of sponsorship of the brewing industry.

Two ages of building are represented here and each occurred at a time of reform and expansion of the university system in Scotland. In the nineteenth century Scottish universities were unique in the sense that they were open to all ranks of society. By the 1860s one-third of the students attending Scottish universities had begun their studies in remote parish schools, which was a far higher proportion than in any other Western country. Scotland was, at this time, therefore, a world leader in the provision of widely available higher education. The Universities (Scotland) Acts of 1858 and 1889 allowed the universities to consolidate their positions, giving them complete independence and allowing for a fair measure of participation by students and staff in the running of the institutions. Edinburgh University was subsequently able to attract increasing numbers of distinguished scholars from all over the world and add to the range of subjects for which it enjoyed an international reputation for excellence. In the twentieth century the universities found themselves accepting ever greater amounts of central government funding and the expansion which took place in the 1960s and early 1970s, of which the new buildings in the photograph were a part, was achieved by this means. Fears were expressed at the time that, despite the fact that the nineteenth-century legislation was still intact, this would lead to a loss of independence from government interference. Recent events have proved these fears justified.

PUBLIC LIBRARY AND THE NATIONAL LIBRARY OF SCOTLAND, EDINBURGH
Below right

This picture depicts a liberality of libraries – at least five separate libraries are in view. The building in the centre-left with the tall pyramidal roof is the Edinburgh Central Public Library of 1887-90. Originally financed, as were many public libraries in Scotland, by Andrew Carnegie, it was a fitting addition to the city in which it is said that the

first circulating library in Britain was set up by the poet Allan Ramsay in the 1720s. The latter was in Parliament Square and might also have been in the photograph had it still been in existence. The large building opposite the Public Library dates from the 1930s and is the National Library of Scotland. This was established in 1925 around a core collection of 750,000 books acquired from the Faculty of Advocates, who had accumulated them since the setting up of the Advocates' Library in 1689. The Advocates' Library itself continued in existence; it retained 45,000 legal books, and is housed in a building which adjoins the National Library and whose dark, slated, pitched roof can just be seen in its shadow. The Advocates' Library is part of the complex of buildings adjacent to St Giles Cathedral (visible top right) which includes the Signet Library (the large building facing the open space next to St Giles), Parliament House (whose five-light medieval window can be seen centre right) and the Solicitors' Library, which is the red sandstone building at lower right. The ground here slopes steeply away from the High Street and most of the buildings have many basement storeys. The Solicitors' Library is in fact the crown of a block of tenements which at its lowest level becomes a row of shops in the Cowgate. The brash modern building in the centre left of the picture is the headquarters of the Lothian Regional Council; this has been described by Colin McWilliam as 'anti-townscape'.

THE ROYAL INFIRMARY OF EDINBURGH

The present Royal Infirmary of Edinburgh was built in 1870-79 to a design by David Bryce. Five hundred beds were provided – Florence Nightingale advised on their layout – in a series of pavilions whose external appearance might be described as 'restrained Scots Baronial'. Bryce was not an architect renowned for his reticence when adding towers, turrets, pinnacles and other fussinesses to buildings but the restraining influence here was a powerful one, and quite normal for this type of building – shortage of money.

The Infirmary is on the southern edge of the Old Town, next to the Meadows, which form a convenient landing-ground for Royal Air Force rescue helicopters. These are fairly regular visitors, usually with civilian casualties of outdoor pursuits on Scottish mountains or coasts.

GLADHOUSE RESERVOIR, MIDLOTHIAN

Gladhouse Reservoir is situated on the principal headwater of the South Esk and is one of several artificial lochs which supply drinking water to Edinburgh. It was constructed in 1878-79 as part of a scheme which was originated to avoid the necessity of drawing water from St Mary's Loch, a well-known beauty spot in the Border hills. The Victorians thus displayed a level of concern for the environment which is all too lacking in the present day, in which the requirement to provide a service which is considered to be 'essential', be it a reservoir, a road or an airport, is frequently used as an excuse for allocating a low priority to the preservation of local amenity.

LADY VICTORIA COLLIERY, NEWTONGRANGE, MIDLOTHIAN

Coal-mining was the main industry in the Lothians in the nineteenth century and Lady Victoria Colliery one of the largest mines; almost 40 million tons of coal were extracted from here between 1894 and 1981, when it was finally closed and became part of the Scottish Mining Museum. The pit was sunk by the Lothian Coal Company, which had assumed responsibility for mining in this area in 1860 from the Marquess of Lothian, whose ancestors had for centuries derived their income from coal. They were descendants of the last abbot of the nearby Abbey of Newbattle, where the monks had been pioneers in the working of coal in Scotland, and were direct, if distant, beneficiaries of the dissolution of the monasteries. The third Marquess achieved notoriety in 1762 as the winner of the famous court case against his own colliers in which the principle of serfdom for coal-workers was established in law.

The Lothian Coal Company built the village of Newtongrange as well as the colliery and this became the largest pit-village in Scotland. As can be seen, it consists of brick-built terraced houses laid out on a grid pattern; each had a flower garden in front, a vegetable garden behind and a dry closet. The threat of eviction from these tied houses was commonly used at Newtongrange by the mine manager, the infamous Mungo Mackay, as a means of forcing the miners to comply with the wishes of the Company.

THE 'FIVE SISTERS' SHALE BING, WEST LOTHIAN

It is not entirely true to say that the world's oil industry began here but it is not so far from being correct. The 'Five Sisters' is a shale bing which was associated with the Addiewell Chemical Works of Young's Paraffin Light and Mineral Oil Company Ltd, founded by James 'Paraffin' Young, a Glasgow-born chemist, who built the world's first oil refinery three miles away at Whiteside in 1848. Using his own patented method to distil oil from coal, he quickly found himself the master of a highly profitable industry which was supplying mineral oil from Whiteside to the United States of America as well as to all parts of Britain. Later, he developed a method for distilling oil products from carboniferous shale – a much cheaper raw material because it had no other use – and it was for this purpose that the Addiewell Works was set up. When Young's patent expired in 1864 others were quick to take advantage of the process and by 1871 over fifty companies were mining shale and producing a total of 25 million gallons of crude oil a year in West Lothian. Scotland was enjoying its first oil boom, but it was to be short-lived (as the second no doubt will be, though for different reasons) because by the 1870s oil had been discovered in America and was available at much lower prices. Young, inventive and business-like as ever, diversified to produce a wide variety of by-products from petroleum jelly and ointment to mothballs, and it was this

spirit which kept the industry alive, though in decline, well into the twentieth century. Shale was last mined in West Lothian in 1962.

The 'Five Sisters' Bing is almost entirely the result of twentieth-century activity and is one of the few reminders of an industry which once employed thousands. It is currently the subject of

controversy between those who wish to see it preserved as a symbol of Victorian enterprise and declared an 'ancient monument', and those who regard it as an 'eyesore', a symbol of a dead industry which should be sold off for use as cheap infill material, thereby vanishing from the landscape.

GALASHIELS, ETTRICK AND LAUDERDALE

In the nineteenth century Galashiels was the centre of the Border tweed-making industry and many of the mills dating from this period can be picked out in this view, as can the River Tweed itself, in the middle distance. The name of the woollen cloth is not in fact derived from that of the river, however, but from an English misreading of 'tweel', a Scots representation of the French word 'tuile'. Galashiels was once on a main railway line, the Waverley Route from Edinburgh to Carlisle – its trackbed runs vertically through the picture – but this was closed in 1969. The town is nevertheless still the home both of a thriving tweed industry and of the Scottish College of Textiles. Melrose and the Eildon Hills are visible in the background.

BRUNTON'S, MUSSELBURGH AND ST MICHAEL'S CHURCHYARD, INVERESK, EAST LOTHIAN

Musselburgh, on the Lothian coast close to Edinburgh, is not normally thought of as a 'steel' town but it is nevertheless the home of Brunton's, which manufactures rope, wire and other special steel components, mainly for aircraft and shipbuilding, but also for civil engineering. Some of the world's largest structures, including the Humber and Bosphorus Bridges, are held aloft on Musselburgh cables. Founded in 1876, the works was greatly expanded in both the First and Second World Wars and is one of the few of Musselburgh's nineteenth-century manufacturing industries to have survived into the late twentieth century.

The steel ropeworks is seen at the top of the picture above the graveyard of St Michael's Church. The house at the bottom was built for another of Musselburgh's wealthy industrialists.

THE GLENKINCHIE DISTILLERY, EAST LOTHIAN

Although the light soils of East Lothian have long been used to produce large quantities of barley, the county is not normally associated with the distilling of whisky. This malt whisky distillery, which is located on the Kinchie Burn a few miles south of Pencaitland, was established by a local farmer in the early years of the nineteenth century. A flavour of the Highlands was added in 1890 when the name Glenkinchie was adopted.

PAPERMILL, RIVER LEVEN, FIFE

Papermaking was an important industry in South-East Scotland in the nineteenth century but the Tullis Russell mill, on the River Leven near Glenrothes, is one of the few survivors. It is an amalgam of two concerns which were each founded in the first decade of the nineteenth century and is currently the largest privately-owned paper manufacturer in Europe.

EYEMOUTH HARBOUR, BERWICKSHIRE

Pictured here is the oldest part of Eyemouth Harbour, a simple, single, riverside quay and one of the few natural harbours on Scotland's inhospitable North Sea coast. It has a long history as both a trading and a fishing port but was probably at its busiest in the nineteenth century when Eyemouth, along with all fishing ports on the East Coast of Scotland, enjoyed the herring fishing boom. During the second half of the century it was the head port in the fishing district extending from St Abb's Head to Amble in Northumberland and on average around 50,000 barrels of herring were cured here annually. It is still one of the busiest fishing ports on the East Coast and one of the few at which fish are actually landed. The fish market – an open-walled shed close to the quayside – is clearly visible in this photograph.

ST MONANCE, FIFE
St Monance, one of the old burghs of the East Neuk of Fife, was another beneficiary of the herring boom of the nineteenth century, and is notable for the fact that its fishermen personally raised the finance to make considerable improvements to their harbour in the 1860s and 1870s. It is also the home of Messrs. J.N. Miller & Sons, one of Scotland's oldest surviving boatbuilders, established in 1747 and still building fishing boats by traditional methods.

LEITH WALK, EDINBURGH

Leith Walk, a country lane which was built up in the nineteenth century, forms a direct link between the port of Leith, at the top of the picture, and the centre of Edinburgh. Leith was for centuries the chief port of Scotland; its sheltered natural harbour and its convenient location for the Baltic and the Low Countries led to increasing foreign trade from the fifteenth century onwards. It should have been an independent Royal Burgh, as many ports with less activity were, but by a series of rather underhand political manoeuvrings in the late sixteenth century, involving monarchs and vice-chancellors among others, it became the property of Edinburgh in 1604. After that, relations between the two communities became embittered because Edinburgh constantly used the revenue from the port as a source of income rather than a means of maintaining and improving the harbour. Independence finally came for Leith in 1833, by which time it was experiencing rapid industrial as well as commercial growth, and the nineteenth century was a period of intense activity for the newly independent parliamentary burgh.

In the eighteenth century rope-, glass- and soap-making had been the main industries but these now gave way to shipbuilding and a wide variety of smaller industries such as brick-making, distilling, tanning and dyeing. The principal export from the port was coal from the Lothian Coalfield and the main imports were timber and grain. Large quantities of wine were also imported, as they had been for centuries, and this trade was joined by that in tea following the breaking of the monopoly of the East India Company, by, among others, the famous Edinburgh and Leith tea merchant, Andrew Melrose.

THE PORT OF LEITH

Until the nineteenth century the harbour at Leith consisted simply of quays flanking the Water of Leith where it widened before passing into the Firth of Forth. As trade expanded in the nineteenth century the single channel became hopelessly congested and by the mid-century new docks had been constructed to the west of the river. Two of these are now filled in, but the entrance to them can be seen at the extreme left of the picture, opposite the white steamship. Dock construction continued throughout the century and the Albert and Edinburgh Docks – top of the picture – had been added by 1881, together with a range of other facilities including graving docks.

Some of Leith's most memorable buildings are visible here. At the extreme bottom of the picture, next to the river, is the former State Cinema – now used for other forms of leisure – which occupies the site of Hawthorn's Engineering Works, a once thriving concern which built steamships and railway locomotives. Melrose's Tea Warehouse is on the opposite bank of the river. On the extreme right can be seen the white walls and red pantiles of Lamb's House, a magnificent specimen of

a seventeenth-century
merchant's house, now
restored. To its left, on
the corner near the
bridge, is the King's
Wark, a seventeenth-
century tenement
complete with traditional
wall-head gable and also
recently restored.
Seaward from this, at the
other end of the Shore, is
the cylindrical Signal
Tower, built originally as
a windmill for making
rape-seed oil, and beyond
it is the rectangular Scots
Baronial bulk of the
former Sailors' Home.

For practically the
whole of the twentieth
century Leith suffered a
decline in both trade and
industry, which led
inevitably to neglected
buildings and derelict
industrial sites, the scars
of which are plainly
visible. In recent years a
measure of prosperity has
returned – there are some
new sheds in the picture –
and with it a resurgence
of civic pride as the
manicured areas of green
and the stone-cleaned
buildings testify.

THE UNION CANAL, FOUNTAINBRIDGE, EDINBURGH

The means of transport initiated by the industrial age came to Edinburgh in the form of the Union Canal, opened in 1822, which linked the city with the Forth and Clyde Canal at Falkirk, and therefore with Glasgow. It was known locally as the 'mathematical river' because it follows the 240-foot contour line all the way from Falkirk and therefore contains no locks. Originally intended to carry mainly sandstone, granite cobbles and slate to the rapidly expanding city, the canal was also used to transport coal and farm produce and provided the fastest means of travelling between Edinburgh and Glasgow. It was at its busiest in the 1820s and 1830s and lost importance following the opening of the Edinburgh and Glasgow Railway in 1842.

The photograph depicts the Lochrin Basin – the canal originally extended as far as Port Hopetoun at Lothian Road – and shows the curious Gilmore Park lifting bridge. The right bank of the basin was formerly occupied by the North British Rubber Works, which was backed by American capital and built in 1856. The present buildings on the site are the Fountain Brewery of Scottish and Newcastle Brewers, built in the 1970s. Several rows of nineteenth-century tenements can be seen at the top of the picture.

THE TAY RAILWAY BRIDGE, FIFE AND TAYSIDE

The Tay Railway Bridge connects Fife with Tayside at Dundee and is Scotland's most notorious structure because its predecessor collapsed during a gale in 1879 taking a train and all aboard to their deaths. In its short life the original bridge, the piers of which are visible in the photograph, had proved to be such a valuable part of Scotland's railway network that the decision was taken immediately to rebuild it and the present structure was opened in 1887.

The first structure was designed by Sir Thomas Bouch, who was ruined by the disaster and whose reputation as an engineer never recovered. The fact that other bridges for which he was responsible, some of which remained in service until the 1960s, were fragile structures which could not carry the heaviest locomotives of the twentieth century, did nothing to endear him to subsequent critics. He has been unjustly treated however. The reasons for the Tay Bridge collapse were complex, and it was the system of management which had evolved in the nineteenth century for the construction and maintenance of large structures which was the real culprit rather than Bouch's design. Bouch did no more nor less at the Tay than was normal for most such enterprises at the time and many of his contemporaries must have said, '. . . there but for the grace of God walk I.' As for the lightness of his other bridges, Bouch was a pioneer in the design of economic structures which contained no more material than was necessary – a concept which is very much part of present-day, as opposed to nineteenth-century, engineering design philosophy. If the structures which were

built by his famous contemporaries are still in service today, carrying much heavier loads than were dreamed of when they were constructed, this would today be considered 'overdesign'. Bouch perhaps was ahead of his time. Catastrophic failures caused by the reduction of factors of safety below the level at which they can compensate for shortcomings in management systems have, sadly, been a fairly common feature of the technological world of the late 1980s, in which car ferries, underground stations, railway trains and airliners have all featured in the melancholy catalogue of reports on disasters. Maybe a return to 'overdesign' is now called for.

THE FORTH RAILWAY BRIDGE, WEST LOTHIAN

THE NORTH BRIDGE AND WAVERLEY STATION, EDINBURGH

The Forth Railway Bridge, opened in 1890, was the final link in the East Coast railway route between London and Aberdeen. It was the first major structure in Britain to be constructed in steel and has come to be regarded as one of the engineering wonders of the world. What many of the tourists who flock to see it every year may not realise, however, is that this huge red object five miles west of Edinburgh had a significant effect on the centre of the city itself, because the increase in traffic which it generated produced chaos both on the congested railway lines to the west of Edinburgh's Waverley Station and in the station itself. The Station and the North Bridge which straddles it were completely rebuilt at the end of the nineteenth century; the station became the largest in the UK, if platform footage is used as the measure, and the new North Bridge became a distinctive part of Edinburgh's townscape. At the same time the rail trackbed was substantially widened and additional tunnels were driven under Calton Hill and the Mound. The price of all this was that the citizens of Edinburgh had to yield up a substantial strip of Princes Street Gardens and come to terms with the intrusion which the increased noise and smoke produced. Opposition from some quarters was fierce, but on this occasion the march of 'progress' was not arrested.

THE LEADERFOOT
VIADUCT, RIVER
TWEED, ETTRICK
AND LAUDERDALE
*The graceful Leaderfoot
Viaduct carried a
single-track branch
railway line across the
River Tweed near
Melrose. Opened in 1865
and long abandoned,
it now forms, for the
romantically inclined, a
significant symbolic
element in the magical
landscape around the
Eildon Hills.*

NORTH BERWICK, EAST LOTHIAN

A Royal Burgh since 1425, North Berwick is situated on the East Lothian coast at the point where the Firth of Forth becomes the North Sea. It was known for a time as the 'Biarritz of the North' but the absence of sunbathing crowds in these pictures, which is probably due to the low air temperature, seems to indicate that this is no longer an appropriate title. Perhaps the wind was warmer in the nineteenth century or maybe people were tougher or maybe it was just that they were not so scantily clad.

Although it was originally a trading and fishing port – the largest buildings in the harbour area are eighteenth-century warehouses – North Berwick developed in the nineteenth century as a fashionable watering place and golfing centre. Following the advent of the railways the town underwent rapid expansion both as a resort and as a place for Edinburgh professionals to live. The population doubled between 1880 and 1905 and 'villa quarters' developed at the west end, close to the railway station. Top architects such as Robert Lorimer and John Kinross were employed to create suitably prestigious dwellings.

MUIRFIELD GOLF COURSE, EAST LOTHIAN

The impeccably maintained Muirfield golf course dates from the very end of the nineteenth century when the Honourable Company of Edinburgh Golfers moved here from Musselburgh Links (reputedly the first golf course in the world). Muirfield is the most exclusive of the many fine courses to be found along the coast of East Lothian and regularly hosts the British Open Championship. The red roofs of the clubhouse are seen at the top of the picture and on its left is Greywalls, a fine Edwardian house and garden – now an hotel – designed by Sir Edwin Lutyens and Gertrude Jekyll respectively.

GREYWALLS, MUIRFIELD AND MUIRFIELD GATE, GULLANE, EAST LOTHIAN

Gullane, like North Berwick, developed in the late nineteenth century as a resort, golfing centre and fashionable place from which to commute to Edinburgh. All three activities were encouraged by the coming of the railway line in 1898 and all three are represented by the buildings depicted here which are fine examples of 'Arts and Crafts' architecture. At the top is Greywalls, by Lutyens and Jekyll, with additions by Robert Lorimer, and reputed to be one of Lutyens' favourites. This was built as a holiday house in 1901 and was used as such by its various owners until becoming an hotel in 1948. The building in the centre is Muirfield clubhouse, opened in 1895. The

house at the bottom of the photograph is Muirfield Gate, built in 1902 by the Edinburgh architect Sydney Mitchell, for his own use.

134

PEEBLES, TWEEDDALE
Peebles was another resort which became fashionable in the nineteenth century, especially following the advent of the railways. The town once boasted two railway stations which served commuters to Edinburgh as well as holiday traffic. The atmosphere was and is one of quiet gentility, especially at the famous Hydropathic Establishment, seen on the extreme right of the picture. This was founded in 1878 although the present building dates from 1905.

TYNECASTLE PARK, EDINBURGH
For those who feel in need of it, an antidote to quiet gentility is a Saturday afternoon spent at the football park. Is it a coincidence therefore that, in its present form, mass spectator sport should have its origins in the Victorian Age? The Heart of Midlothian Football Club, an Edinburgh institution, was founded in 1874 and the present ground at Tynecastle, which is depicted here, was officially opened in 1886. The photograph was taken on a bright October afternoon in 1988 when the crowd, which must have approached the stadium's present capacity of 29,000, watched the home team play Glasgow Celtic. The largest attendance ever recorded here was in 1932 when an astonishing 53,396 people watched Hearts play Rangers. Although a capacity crowd is now a rarity the 'game' is nevertheless in a healthy state in West Edinburgh in the heart of what was at one time a Victorian suburb.

EDINBURGH SPRING

I walk my paint-box suburb. The clear air
Is flecked with green and ultramarine and rose.
The wind hangs nursery rhymes on branches;
The sun leans ladders against the apple trees.

And all my defence against the advancing summer
Is to trim hedges, gush the gutters sweet,
Tie the doomed rose against the wall
And watch myself being young and innocent.

Trams from my innocence thunder by like suns
Through my familiar city to where I know
Slatternly tenements wait till night
To make a Middle Ages in the sky.

A buzzing gas-lamp there must be my rose
Eating itself away in the ruined air
Where a damp bannister snakes up and
Time coughs his lungs out behind a battered door.

There craggy windows blink, mad buildings toss,
Dishevelled roofs, and dangerous shadows lean
Heavy with centuries, against the walls;
And Spring walks by ashamed, her eyes cast down.

She's not looked at. O merry midnight when
Squalid Persepolis shrugs its rotting stone
Round in its old bones and hears the crowds
Weeping and cheering and crying, 'Tamburlaine'.

VII

THE TWENTIETH CENTURY

THE FIRST half of the twentieth century, especially the 1920s and 1930s, was a time of decline in Scottish industry and of little change in agriculture, so neither industry nor agriculture produced significant alterations in the landscape in this period. The need for houses was still pressing, however, and the city of Edinburgh continued to expand. Large public housing estates, such as Craigmillar, and private developments, such as the spread of bungalows in Corstorphine, significantly increased the physical area occupied by the city. The trend continued in the 1950s and 1960s as so-called 'slum clearance' programmes caused large numbers of soundly built Victorian tenement houses to be demolished in the city centre. The communities which were destroyed were moved to new housing schemes in Pilton and Wester Hailes and to the sterile environment of architectural 'Modernism' within which the effective rebuilding of communities proved to be extremely difficult to achieve. Thus, new slums were created, despite the best of intentions on the part of all concerned, and these contributed to producing as many, if not more, social problems than they were intended to solve.

The post-Second World War period was also the age in which the modern human love affair with the motor car significantly affected both landscape and townscape. South-East Scotland was perhaps less affected by this than many other areas of the UK but nevertheless by now has its share of motorways, bypasses and relief roads, each with its crop of dead-space around roundabouts and road junctions. The decline of the High Street – that erstwhile centre of the community – is also represented by the appearance of retailers' sheds – 'superstores' – which have sprung up around the newly created traffic arteries. Roads and sheds have become prominent features in the landscape of the late twentieth century. These stand out particularly strongly in the view from the air, partly because of the highly artificial nature of their forms, and also due to their scale relative to that of other structures.

The centre of Edinburgh has not been left untouched by all this recent 'progress'. Princes Street and the area around George Square, for example, have been completely transformed. Many of the open spaces which were created by the 'slum' demolitions of the 1950s and 1960s remained unfilled for many years – serving as muddy carparks – and are only now being slowly built up, frequently with housing developments which attempt, with varying degrees of success, to re-create what was lost during the slum clearance programmes. Would it not have been better to have restored the original buildings?

Some sites were developed for other purposes, however, the most prominent of these being that of the eighteenth-century St James Square, upon which Edinburgh's largest lump of exposed concrete, the

St James Centre, was erected. This is a monument to two of the twentieth century's greatest gods, Mammon and Bureaucracy, and its form very adequately expresses the materialistic world-view of its creators. The forms of Modernist architecture are merely a physical expression of the principal beliefs and priorities of the present day. As has often been said, a culture engenders the architecture which it deserves. Future changes in our priorities will presumably be accompanied by different human influences on our environment.

BUNGALOWS, CORSTORPHINE, EDINBURGH

Bungaloid, bungalurbia, bungalomania, bungal architecture; bungalows were privately developed mass-produced houses, built mainly in the period between the two World Wars and they brought individual home-ownership of a detached house within the grasp of former tenement and terrace dwellers. The house-type was based on those of the British nabobs in India during the period of the Raj, and, although somewhat different from the traditional Scottish cottage, had some of the aura of the English Arts and Crafts type of cottagey houses which were being built for well-off professionals in places such as Gullane, North Berwick and the 'superior' suburbs of Edinburgh. As buildings the bungalows were too small to create significant townscape and Corstorphine has been described by John Gifford in the Edinburgh volume of The Buildings of Scotland *as '. . . the epitome of urban sprawl, cut off by golf courses from direct contact with its parent town'.*

139

FLATS, RAVELSTON GARDENS, EDINBURGH

Proving that Edinburgh was in touch with the very latest architectural ideas in the 1930s, these flats, which date from 1935-37, were among the first buildings to bring the International Style to the city. Slightly nautical in appearance, they had the attributes which the great architectural guru Le Corbusier would have thought appropriate for modern living. They were white-painted, with suites of interconnecting rooms, and they were equipped with the latest gadgetry, such as service lifts, and had roof gardens and servants' quarters. We find ourselves here in the world of cloche hats, limousines and sun terraces: the architectural epitome of 'fastness'.

COUNCIL HOUSING SCHEME, CRAIGMILLAR, EDINBURGH

'Sun, space, verdure . . .' were for Le Corbusier, who was portrayed, and who also portrayed himself, as a Man of Vision ' . . . the magisterial shield of the conditions of nature . . .' within which the modern metropolis must be constructed. His ideas, which were not new although the vocabulary was (similar thoughts had occurred to the builders of Edinburgh's New Town for similar reasons) were obviously shared by the architects of the City Architect's Department who planned the Craigmillar housing scheme illustrated here (built 1930-34), which was occupied by families displaced by slum clearance programmes in the city centre. The buildings have a mildly traditional flavour (Le Corbusier would have built tower blocks) and were acceptable by the standards of the time, but the area subsequently acquired an unenviable reputation as a generator of seemingly intractable social problems. Critics complained that no facilities other than churches or schools were provided. It is certainly true that little attempt was made to provide any of the more subtle components which make up the amenity of a satisfying place to live. Space and light were not enough.

HOUSING AT
SILVERKNOWES,
EDINBURGH
*A mixture of private and
public housing is depicted
here, dating from the
1920s and 1930s, and
clearly inspired by
Ebenezer Howard's
Garden City Movement,
a late-nineteenth-century
vision of Utopia.*

HOUSING AND PLAYGROUND SCULPTURE, CRAIGMILLAR, EDINBURGH

The housing shown here, which is in the Niddry Marischal area of Craigmillar, dates from the late 1960s and was, at that time, the subject of an architectural award. There is, however, little sign of life in the photographs because most of the houses are now abandoned and boarded up. Broken glass and other debris crunch under the feet of any pedestrians who venture out and burnt-out cars block the underpasses which were intended to separate them from motorised traffic. The causes of this situation are obviously complex; a rehabilitation scheme is at present underway to restore the houses to occupancy.

The concrete playground figure was built as part of a community arts project.

143

WESTER HAILES, EDINBURGH

Wester Hailes, Edinburgh's most recent large-scale area of public housing, was built in the 1960s by the City's Corporation, who believed that the creation of a new suburb was the only feasible way to reduce the growing waiting-list for houses. Great hopes were entertained for this new development. Blocks of flats rather than individual houses were built so as to provide the required number of dwellings and still leave open space for light and greenery. They were grouped into squares and quadrangles in an attempt to create communities. Pedestrians were separated from motor traffic according to the dogma of the day, and the Union Canal and a small river which runs through the site were piped and buried so that children could theoretically play in safety. Schools and a community centre were provided and there was also a plan to have a corner shop for every 300 houses, although this did not, unfortunately, materialise.

From the air, the place looks neat and tidy, if a little institutional; at ground level today Wester Hailes is plagued with many social problems although lively community efforts are being made to solve them. The scheme demonstrated the fairly obvious truth that there is a great deal more to the creation of thriving and healthy communities than separating pedestrians from traffic and filling in canals. In fact the kind of thinking which regards these expedients as solutions, based as it is on reason without intuition, might even be one of the root causes of the failure.

RECENT HOUSING, CORSTORPHINE, EDINBURGH

Below

'Since 1920 Corstorphine has been the speculative builder's demesne', wrote John Gifford in the Edinburgh volume of The Buildings of Scotland. *These are among the most recent examples of the art of building for profit and they show that an effort has been made to provide more imaginative layouts than those of the 1930s versions nearby. Trees and shrubs are more plentiful here than in the near contemporary Wester Hailes, but neither vegetation nor irregular planning can alleviate the monotony of building forms which are controlled by the laws of economics rather than by those which determine how true 'places' are created.*

144

'HERITAGE' HOMES, LEITH

The alternating red and blue tiled roofs of recently built 'heritage' homes – sanitised versions of an East Neuk of Fife fishing village – occupy the centre of this photograph. Their presence among converted and restored older buildings in the much-tidied-up heart of Leith suggests that after half a century of neglect and declining property values the ancient port has become a place in which a certain type of lifestyle associated with the 1980s is now possible, all under the protection of good 'Queen Margaret's' nuclear umbrella, seen represented at the top of the photograph.

*The massive development
in the foreground is
Edinburgh's largest lump
of exposed concrete. It
houses a shopping centre,
an hotel, New St
Andrew's House (the
home of the Scottish
Office) and a multi-storey
car park. The monuments
on Calton Hill are seen
behind.*

*The curious geometric
pattern in the centre of
this photograph is made
by the roof lights,
planting and walkways
on top of Edinburgh's
underground shopping
centre at the Waverley
Market. Some people feel
that this may well be the
best angle from which to
view it, although the
building is usually filled
with enthusiastic patrons
of its speciality shops.
Such developments are
distantly related to the
grand shopping arcades of
some nineteenth-century
city centres but most of
them lack the scale and
the high quality of
materials and finishes
which made the originals
so successful.*

'SAVACENTRE',
CAMERON TOLL,
EDINBURGH
This is Edinburgh's largest shopping shed to date, part of the 'motor culture'; motor cars and motor buses are required for shopping, motor lorries to replenish the shed and motorways for all of them to drive on. This and similar centres around the perimeter of the city have altered shopping patterns, all but destroying its suburban high streets. An advantage of the system which supports the supersheds is that seasonal commodities such as tomatoes and strawberries can now be bought all year round; other disadvantages are that it is sometimes difficult to distinguish the taste of one from the other, and that large areas of town and countryside have been covered with tarmacadam.

MOTORWAY,
WEST LOTHIAN
*This is the embankment
which carries the road
which carries the lorries
which carry the watery,
tasteless, polythene-
forced, non-organically-
grown, imported
tomatoes to the
supermarket sheds.*

SMALL BUSINESS
UNITS,
GLENROTHES, FIFE
Overleaf
*These small business units
(sheds again, this time of
the multicoloured
'Smartie' variety) are
among the most recent
additions to Glenrothes,
one of Britain's most
successful New Towns.
The Glenrothes
Development
Corporation was set up in
1948 under the New
Towns Act of 1946 and
building work began in
1951. The town is not
based on any existing
community nor was it
tied to any single industry
and the second of these
especially may account for
its success in the second
half of the twentieth
century. By the 1980s it
had become a thriving
centre for a variety of
'white collar' industries
and is also the
administrative centre of
Fife; the Fife Regional
Health Board and all of
the departments of Fife
Regional Council are
based here.*

149

OIL PLATFORM CONSTRUCTION YARD, BUCKHAVEN, FIFE

Buckhaven was one of a small number of towns in Scotland which benefited directly from the second oil boom of the 1970s and 1980s. Built on the site of a colliery which had closed in 1967, this yard, which dates from 1979, brought much-needed employment to a depressed area. The Lomond Hills can be seen in the background of the photograph behind the intensively worked agricultural landscape of Fife.

COCKENZIE POWER STATION, EAST LOTHIAN

There is no evidence of smoke here from the twin chimneys of Cockenzie Power Station. Despite the grey sea and sky, this photograph, which looks westwards towards Edinburgh, depicts a summer scene in 1988, when a chill wind was already blowing through the Scottish coal industry, with which Cockenzie has long been associated.

The very first railway in Scotland (strictly speaking a waggonway) was built here in 1722 to link coal-mines at Tranent with the small harbour (just visible under the power station), but long before that Cockenzie had been a coal and salt community which exported both commodities to the Low Countries.

The power station is one of a number on the shores of the Firth of Forth which have been served by the local mines, now much threatened by cheap imported coal, political dogma, and expensive nuclear power. In 1947 Scotland had 237 collieries which employed 81,000 miners. By the 1960s the workforce had fallen to 50,000. In 1989, in the wake of the 1984 confrontation between the miners and an unsympathetic government, only three working pits were left, two of which supplied Cockenzie, and the number of miners had fallen to 2,200.

WESTFIELD OPENCAST COALMINE, FIFE

The very first coal workings were no doubt of the opencast type, making use of outcropping seams. Modern opencast mines operate on shallow seams and use earth-moving machinery to strip off the over-burden and to quarry the coal beneath. The visual impact on the environment is very great while the works are in progress. After the coal has been removed, however, it is possible to fill in the hole and return the land successfully to agriculture. Backfilling is in progress here at Westfield in Fife, one of a number of opencast sites in South-East Scotland.

154

TORNESS POWER STATION AND DUNGLASS COLLEGIATE CHURCH, EAST LOTHIAN

Scotland has a surplus of generating capacity and is a net exporter of electricity, which caused many people to question the wisdom of building a nuclear power station in East Lothian. More than one kind of power was involved, of course. Yet another kind is represented by the fifteenth-century collegiate church of Dunglass, in the foreground of the photograph. This was last used as a church in the seventeenth century but the building subsequently served as a barn and a stable and is now simply one of the many interesting ruins which can be visited in East Lothian. It is therefore a building for which some use has always been found.

There will be no question of Torness Power Station fulfilling a similar diversity of functions once its generating days are over. It is a sobering thought that societies as distant from ours into the future as those who built the henge on Cairnpapple Hill are in the past, will have to concern themselves with the guarding and proper management of the lethal waste products from our nuclear power stations, and of certain parts of the power stations themselves, whether on the original site or following removal to some 'remote' nuclear dump.

155

OIL REFINERY, GRANGEMOUTH, FALKIRK

Grangemouth, which is Scotland's only major petrochemical complex, is not flattered by the weather conditions in this photograph although it does give an indication of the output of pollutants to the atmosphere. The first plant was built here in 1924, by Scottish Oils, which was an amalgam of the surviving West Lothian oil shale companies, and its purpose was to process oil from the Persian Gulf. The writing was clearly on the wall for the locally mined raw material.

Today a greatly expanded Grangemouth is linked directly by pipeline to the new oilfields of the northern North Sea. Nevertheless, only a modest proportion of the output from the Scottish sector is actually processed here. Most of the Scottish crude oil is exported as such, to be refined elsewhere.

FENTON BARNS, EAST LOTHIAN

In the 1830s, at the height of the period of agricultural 'improvement', George Hope, the enterprising tenant of Fenton Barns, set up a small factory for making drainage tiles and was able to finance the drainage and levelling of his own fields out of the profits of selling these to his neighbours. The nineteenth-century farmhouse and a number of cottages are visible in this photograph, as is the original steading, though the latter is almost buried within a cluster of large modern sheds used for the intensive rearing of livestock – a twentieth-century factory at Fenton Barns. The new buildings, like the old, are purely functional and without embellishments; unlike the old they are not made principally from local materials and bear no trace of local character. The forms of the sheds of modern agribusiness are similar to those used by manufacturing industry and commerce; they are generally monotonous and brutal, but then so are many of the activities which are carried on within them.

FIELDS AND THE RIVER TYNE, EAST LOTHIAN

Overleaf
This photograph illustrates something of the care and trouble which is taken in the working of the precious arable land of East Lothian.

157

FIELD OF RAPE, EAST LOTHIAN

The dazzling field of yellow oilseed rape has become a prominent feature of the early summer landscape of South-East Scotland. Rape has in fact been grown for many years in the UK, most recently as a break crop within intensive cereal systems, but it became very common in the 1980s due to the setting of attractive support prices by the European Economic Community so as to increase production of vegetable oils and protein meals within Europe. The phenomenon is an example of the effect which decisions taken by government authorities have on the farming community and hence on the appearance of the countryside. Since the passing of the British Agricultural Act of 1947, in which a system of guaranteed prices was introduced for farm produce, farming in the UK has been increasingly directed by the policies of successive governments and their advisers, and this trend has continued following Britain's entry into the EEC. Although the issue is obviously a very complex one, the fact that obesity is now thought to be a greater threat to the health of the population of Britain than is malnutrition might perhaps be taken as an indication of the success of agriculture under these policies. Other effects have also occurred, however. Land prices have been artificially increased and this has encouraged a very large investment of capital in agriculture.

The consequences have been momentous. Farming is now highly technological; the application of artificially produced chemicals to the land takes place on a vast scale and the removal of plant forms, such as hedges and trees, which compete with crops, is encouraged. All of these are potentially environmentally damaging in the long term and, in the case of pesticides and artificial fertilisers, follow a law of diminishing returns. Mechanised farming has reduced the need for labour and continued the depopulation of rural areas which began in the first Agricultural Revolution. The machines used in modern farming are very large, which has made the old buildings obsolete and led, in many cases, to their replacement by the ubiquitous shed, which, however necessary, is seldom a visually pleasing addition to the landscape.

The visual, social and environmental effects of 'agribusiness' on the countryside have therefore been considerable and many of them may be discerned in this photograph. The lack of hedges and trees is obvious, as is the preponderance of modern sheds in the farm to the right of the yellow field. Less obvious are the effects of artificial chemicals on the landscape; the uniformity of the field colours results mainly from the application of pesticides and herbicides and the deep shades of green from the use of nitrogenous fertilisers. Most of the dwellings in the picture are no longer occupied by farm workers. The landscape here is bureaucratic agricultural policy translated into visual form and it is the latest of the several attempts at the domination of both humans and nature which are evident in the background of this photograph.

THE BASS ROCK, EAST LOTHIAN

Below left

The Bass Rock, off the East Lothian coast, has featured in a minor way throughout Scottish history. The hermit St Baldred is said to have lived here in the eighth century and the castle, which was built in the sixteenth century, has been used as a prison at various times. Covenanting ministers were incarcerated here in the seventeenth century and a band of Jacobite prisoners once took possession of it, after overcoming the garrison, and were able to hold out for a period of three years, leading a semi-piratical existence by raiding passing merchant ships and the mainland for provisions. Today the Rock is uninhabited – the lighthouse is now automatic – and is a semi-wilderness colonised by seabirds which are thriving in an environment relatively untouched by human activity. The craggy, volcanic form of the Rock and the vitality of the wildlife around it, are in stark contrast to the intensively farmed, gently rolling landscape of adjacent East Lothian. The most numerous of the seabirds are the Gannets, whose Latin name Sula bassana is derived from the Bass, and who render the cliffs an intense white during the summer months of the breeding season. The island also supports colonies of Fulmars, Kittiwakes, Greater and Lesser Black-Backed Gulls, Herring Gulls, Guillemots, Razorbills, Shags, Cormorants and Puffins.

LANDSCAPE NEAR SELKIRK, ETTRICK AND LAUDERDALE

In this landscape, in which all the planting is artificial, a nice balance is achieved between farming and forestry. Such landscapes, especially if more broadleaved trees are included than are seen here, can provide a variety of habitats for wildlife as well as materials for human consumption. It seems possible that the more intensively farmed parts of the countryside will gradually be returned to such mixed land use in the future as measures designed to prevent the continued creation of food mountains by the use of 'high-tech' farming take effect. The lowland landscape will then become 'healthier' as well as more pleasing visually.

HEATHER BURNING PATTERNS, LAMMERMUIR HILLS, EAST LOTHIAN

The Lammermuir Hills are used today mainly for sheep grazing but are also managed as grousemoors. Heather is burned so as to clear areas for new growth and the pattern of the burnt patches depends on the direction of the wind. The mosaic-like forms in this photograph are the result of successive years of burning, the black areas being the most recently burned, and the dark brown the mature growth of tall, old heather.

CRAMOND VILLAGE, EDINBURGH

Cramond, which is now part of Edinburgh, is a coastal village with a long history. The Romans, under the Emperor Antonius Pius, built a harbour and fort here in the second century AD, as part of the frontier line across Scotland from Forth to Clyde. It was a substantial settlement which included facilities for ironworking, tanning and shoemaking. In the seventeenth century the river was lined with corn mills and in the eighteenth, Cramond had its own industrial revolution when it became a local centre of the iron industry. In its heyday, in the last two decades of the century, 300 tons of rod iron for nails of all types were made here annually, although the iron was never actually smelted at Cramond; it was imported in the form of bar iron from Russia, Holland and other parts of Britain. This industry became extinct in the nineteenth century – traces of the industrial buildings can still be seen on the river banks – following which Cramond became a quiet backwater until the advent of the motor car made it accessible both as a residential suburb of Edinburgh and as a place of recreational boating, roles which it continues to play today.

ANSTRUTHER, FIFE

In the nineteenth century Anstruther was at the centre of the Scottish herring fishing industry. At that time large shoals of fish used to appear annually in the Firth of Forth and Scottish fishermen would base themselves at Anstruther from January until March; at such times it was possible apparently to walk from one side of the harbour to the other by stepping from boat to boat. Since the Second World War fishing has dwindled; it is said that the shoals have deserted their traditional waters. Perhaps they simply no longer exist, in obedience to cycles of abundance and scarcity caused by factors in the natural ecology of the herring. Perhaps, like the whale, their numbers were depleted by over-intense fishing during the 'boom' years of the industry.

Tourism has replaced fishing as the principal means of livelihood in most of the coastal towns of the East Neuk of Fife and recently it was decided that Anstruther should no longer have any active fishing boats (the survivors will in future work from Pittenweem where new harbour works are planned) but should become the local centre of the 'Heritage Industry'. The Scottish Fisheries Museum was opened here in 1969, in a group of buildings which have for centuries been associated with fishing, and it is this which now attracts shoals of visitors annually. The museum possesses a fine collection of boats, some of which are large vessels displayed in the harbour, which they share with the North Carr Lightship, a maritime antique now permanently moored here, but which was once stationed at sea close by, off Fife Ness.

RIDING ON
BELHAVEN BEACH,
EAST LOTHIAN
*Riders slow their horses
to a walk after an
exhilarating gallop along
Belhaven Beach, one of
the longest unbroken
stretches of sand on the
East Lothian coast.*

EDINBURGH'S
OLDEST AND
NEWEST BUILDINGS
*The single cell of
St Margaret's Chapel in
Edinburgh Castle is
Edinburgh's oldest
building. The white tent
covering the Ross
Bandstand in Princes
Street Gardens is
annually its newest. Each
can represent the cultural
values of the age to which
it belongs.*

EDINBURGH ON A
LATE WINTER
AFTERNOON JUST
BEFORE CHRISTMAS
*A view up the High
Street towards the castle.
The Christmas tree on
the Mound stands out in
white, the red star burns
atop the City Chambers,
and a green light
illumines the Head Office
of the Bank of Scotland.*

167

DAYBREAK

Count the lights down,
those lustrous, trembling stars.

If there's an hour whose father
was Proteus, this is it.

The night sky is turning into
a space of pearl. In the East

it faintly flushes, where the hidden sun
sends forward its gentle announcement.

And history, that hasn't slept, yawns
in his workshop – he'll make

a million things today
and be surprised by none of them.

There's one already – a milk bottle waiting
for the door of a house to open.

And another – a baby crying
in the first of all its minutes.